THE CAMPAIGN IN INDIA

Illustrations by George Francklin Atkinson

First published by Day and Son, Lithographers to the Queen,
Gare Street, Lincoln Inn Fields, 1 January 1859

Royal Armouries facsimile reprint 2009

Introductory essay by
Simon Riches
Education Department, Royal Armouries Museum

It is hard to avoid George Francklin Atkinson's iconic imagery of India. Plates from The Campaign in India: *1857–58 are standards on the 'Indian Mutiny' menu, their distinct texture adding substance to a wide variety of texts. This edition affords the opportunity to once more offer the book in the manner Captain Atkinson intended it to be read. His biography is as illuminating as his illustrations and this volume pencils in the finer details of a life only previously sketched.*

ROYAL▪ARMOURIES

Royal Armouries Museum
Armouries Drive
Leeds LS10 1LT

© 2009 The Trustees of the Armouries
First published 2009

ISBN 978 0 948092 63 3

Printed in Great Britain by BAS Fine Art Printers, Amesbury, Wiltshire

INTRODUCTION

George Francklin Atkinson was born in Calcutta on 8 May 1822.[1] The fourth of five sons born to James Atkinson, the family comprised soldier, surgeon, engineer and clergyman. In common with their mother Jane Bathie, at least four of the sons were born and baptised in Calcutta. Their surgeon father and pioneering Persian scholar was the only member of the family born in England, in County Durham on 9 March 1780.[2] James studied medicine at Edinburgh and London and took a position as surgeon's mate on the Honourable East India Company ship *Lord Duncan* in 1802. After a period of home service as a surgeon in England, he was appointed to the Bengal Medical Establishment on 23 May 1805 at Calcutta.[3]

His first posting found him in charge of the station at Bakarganj near Barisal and by 1812 he had gravitated South to Madras to act as superintending surgeon.[4] His first son Robert James Atkinson was born on 23 March 1812 and his imminent promotion to Assistant Assay Master at the Calcutta Mint hastened his return to the North and marriage to Jane on 14 October 1815.[5]

As James and Jane laid the foundations of the family, their stock slowly increased. Frederick Dayot Atkinson was born on 23 July 1816 and Charles D'Oyly Atkinson (born in 1818) was baptised at Fort William, Calcutta on 21 April 1821.[6] By this time James had become superintendent of the *Government Gazette,* held the deputy chair of Persian at Fort William College and published the first English translation of part of the famous *Shah-nama* (book of kings) of Firdawsi of Tus.[7] James as author looked to the distant past to find reflections of the classical world mirrored in the Persian scripts of the language of the learned. James as editor looked back to Europe through the lens of an expatriate community, distorted by twenty years of heat and longing for home. It was to England that the family returned in 1825.

The East India Company ship *Princess Charlotte of Wales* left for England in December 1825.[8] On board were the Atkinson and Sneyd families. Robert James was thirteen, Frederick Dayot nine, Charles D'Oyly seven and George Francklin three. If the Atkinson brothers could barely imagine the approaching winter shores of England, then the Sneyd family could still less conceive the kiln hot climate of crisis they would face in 1857. Elizabeth Sneyd produced a vivid account of her families experience in India, but in 1825 her thoughts must have been with her absent husband Captain Edward Carncross Sneyd, en route to East India Company territory in Burma, not cast 32 years into the future and a desperate flight through Cawnpore to Calcutta.[9] The young Anna Sneyd's paranoid dreams of *'being killed in a church by black-skinned-men'* did not provide sufficient clairvoyance to foresee the drowning of her father off the coast of Burma a year later or their own shipwreck in 1853.[10] Nor did she predict the elemental destruction of Charles Metcalfe Sneyd who perished beneath froth and flame as his Benares steamer burned and sank beneath the waves in 1847. The demise of her beloved sister Alice Caroline Sneyd in 1856 from 'feverish attack' was not heralded by visions or omens.[11] Both Anna and her brother Captain Henry Wilder Sneyd did indeed flee the barricaded church at Shajahanpur only to be killed near Aurangabad in June 1857, but the spectres of disease and drowning had already carried away more of the Sneyd family than revolt and rebellion.[12] These events were far over the horizon in 1825 and if apprehension was felt by anyone, it was acute in the young Atkinson brothers approaching the start of their schooldays in a country they barely knew.

As Atkinson senior travelled between England and India, his sons set out on divergent educational journeys. Whilst Robert James followed his father into the medical profession,[13] Frederick Dayot endured Greek, Latin and maths *'under Mr Griffiths at Boulogne'*[14] and Charles D'Oyly took classics and mathematics at Bury St Edmunds with the sinister sounding Dr Firmingers.[15] This preparatory education primed them for Addiscombe, the East India Company's military seminary near Croydon. Addiscombe demanded that each candidate *'possess a correct knowledge of all the rules of arithmetic usually taught in schools'* and further required an ability *'to construe and parse Caesars commentaries correctly'* before admission could be approved. Not that parents should worry as *'the youth whose parent or friend may place him there, has the satisfaction of knowing that, even if his indolence of deficient natural capacity prevent his obtaining a superior Cadetship, he is still sure of his Infantry appointment, and may at some later period turn his modicum of acquired knowledge to account'.* A further desiderata was appended - *'it is also very desirable that a Cadet, on joining the Seminary, be able to draw with facility in pencil, and shade with Indian ink',* a skill which the dexterous George Francklin was keen to demonstrate.[16]

George Francklin Atkinson received his classical and mathematical education at Kensington Proprietary Grammar and was nominated to the seminary by William Wigram at the recommendation of Money Wigram on 5 December 1838.[17] The Company Court of Directors and Board of Control appointed officer cadets on a personal basis, each having a fixed quota per annum. Both Frederick Dayot and Charles D'Oyly had been nominated by company director James Stuart after recommendations from their father in 1831 and 1832 respectively.[18] As Stuart had been dead five years and James Atkinson was now Chief Surgeon to the Army of the Indus and about to cross into Afghanistan in pursuit of Dost Mahommed Khan the rebellious Emir of Kabul, this proved slightly more difficult for the youngest son. The Wigram family owned the vitally important Blackwall shipyard and exerted considerable influence in the East India Company. Their nomination indicates the circles within which the Atkinson family circulated, a small company of actors which welcomed well-connected characters to the stage for mutual advancement.

When George Francklin Atkinson began his career at Addiscombe, his older brothers had already entered service. Robert James Atkinson became a member of the Royal College of Surgeons in 1834, six years before his own father.[19] James Atkinson senior was probably preoccupied with the early years of his youngest and newest son James Augustus (born circa 1831) to worry about his career at that precise moment in time. Frederick Dayot Atkinson was promoted to adjutant of the newly raised '2nd Bengal European Regiment' on 13 December 1839[20] and Charles D'Oyly entered service as an ensign with the 40th Native Infantry at Sagar in 1836.[21] Charles finally married his heavily pregnant wife Harriet Maria Bunbury on 28 October 1839 and their daughter Jane Harriet Atkinson was born at Dinapore on 7 December 1840.[22] It didn't say anything about *that* in his father's joint work with his namesake Sir Charles D'Oyly of 1825 – *Tom Raw, The Griffin: A Burlesque Poem in Twelve Cantos!* A young cadet was known as a 'griff' or 'griffin' and their 'Adventures of a Cadet in the East India Company's Service' were 'equally excellent and entertaining', commencing 'with the period of the cadet quitting England' and concluding 'with his attaining staff appointment'. Accordingly, 'a number of ludicrous events and scenes are narrated; and our Indian friends will recognise many real characters who are admirably sketched to the life'.[23] This is a clear influence on George Francklin Atkinson's colourful *Curry and Rice* though *Tom Raw* carried far less heat than the 40 plates offered up in 1858.[24]

As the young George Francklin carefully laid out his new regulation equipment of 'jackets, waistcoats, stocks, foraging caps, trousers, shoes, gloves.... twelve shirts (including three nightshirts), eight pair of cotton-stockings; six ditto, worsted ditto; six towels; six night-caps; eight pocket handkerchiefs; one pair of white trousers; a tooth brush; a Bible and Prayer book; a case of mathematical instruments of an approved pattern' the volume of which was 'considered by the Military Committee to be necessary', his father was busily being robbed blind at Kyhrpur on his journey to Afghanistan.[25] Waking at five on the morning of 7 February 1839 James Atkinson observed that 'the whole had disappeared: wearing apparel, shaving apparatus, writing-case, with all my memoranda, lists, receipts, letters, spectacles, sketchbooks, journal, and a variety of small trifles, but important considering the impossibility of replacing them on march'. His 'annoyance and vexation at the loss of my drawings and papers was extreme' and conjectured that the anxiety he frequently expressed over their safety, led the more acquisitive of his companions to the conclusion that his paper-case contained money.[26] James' account and colour lithographs (published separately) are important in terms of military history as he was one of the few survivors of the expedition. They are important in terms of the biography of George Francklin Atkinson as they underline the importance of his influence on the young artist. Both produced serious work alongside caricature, though Atkinson junior would certainly outdo his father in the latter.

It was most likely artistic skill with pen and pencil that separated him from both his older infantry brothers and fellow cadets. Senior cadetships in the Artillery and Engineers were most sought after and if his brothers only managed infantry appointments, George Francklin must have been pleased to be 'presented with the Fortification & Civil Drawing Prizes of the 2nd Class at the Public Examination of the 11th June and with the 1st Fortification Prizes of the 1st Class on 11th Dec. 1840, the day on which he passed Public Examination'.[27] The day's events were recorded in detail by *The United Service Journal and Naval and Military Magazine*:

'The proceedings of the day [Thursday] began in the Fortification Department by the formation of a light bridge for infantry, made of a pair of long spars, resting on two of Blanchard's small infantry pontoons, the roadway being covered with hurdles. As soon as this was dismantled, a bridge was rapidly prepared and tried for the passage of light artillery... two neat suspension bridges... two charges of gunpowder of ten and fifteen pounds respectively were sunk in water five and six deep; these were fired simultaneously by Professor Daniell, who was present with his voltaic battery: the result was perfect, and the effect beautiful - the domes of water rising to a height of about twenty five feet. In an adjoining field, a gate was prepared in a rough parapet, against the bottom of which a bag of gunpowder, containing forty pounds was laid; its explosion blew down the gate, and opened a passage for three or four men to pass in abreast, thus illustrating the operation at Ghuznee.'[28]

James Atkinson was present at the taking of Ghuznee nearly a year earlier in July 1839. He saw the gates collapse under a charge at least three times larger than that used at Addiscombe, treated in vain the dysentery that 'no age escaped and no rank' and endured earthquakes, whirlwinds and scorching heat, all conditions Addiscombe could scarcely replicate.[29] Yet the relevance of this demonstration would not be lost on his young cadet son. These were skills he could expect to use and were talents his fellow engineers employed almost to the letter in their destruction of the Kashmiri gate at Delhi on 14 September 1857. As the day wore on an inspection of the Military Drawing Department singled out *'the principal drawings'* which included his work on *'Tarragone'* (presumably the 1813 Siege of Tarragona). A visit to the Landscape Department revealed that *'as usual we found much to admire'* including *'a well executed drawing of cattle and figures by Cadet G. Atkinson'* and *'many excellent specimens of lithographic skill were displayed, evincing considerable improvement in this very useful department, among which we particularly noticed those of.... Atkinson'*. As dusk fell *'Mr Angelo's sword exercise, and the usual salute of 15 guns, fired by Cadets, closed the business of the day'*. He had done well and it was hoped that Addiscombe and its officers would *'produce many efficient Engineers for the Company's Service, at a period of our Indian Empire when military science is more likely to be in demand than at any previous epoch of its martial and eventful annals'*.[30]

George Francklin's time at Addiscombe was well spent, so carefully measured in fact that in 1848 he was *'entitled to sanction one year ten months and ten days, the time passed at the seminary after attaining the age of sixteen, as so much time passed in, for retirement on full pay'*.[31] This was the precise amount of time he had spent at the seminary and effectively meant the Company was prepared to pay *him* for attending *their* school and let him retire early to boot! How he managed this is not entirely clear, though if Addiscombe had at least produced one Engineer cadet in the shape of George Francklin Atkinson his training was not over yet.

From 1815 the Company sent successful cadets to the Royal Engineers Establishment at Chatham for training in sapping and mining. It was here he arrived as 'temporary Ensign' on 1 February 1841.[32] He acquired a new set of brothers, aspirant Engineer officers with whom he would be recorded throughout his career. The individual numbering of soldiers was some way off but George Francklin Atkinson, Archibald Impey, James Pattle Beadle, Reginald John Walker and Thomas Charles Phillpotts were numbered '436' as a group in the Bengal Service Army Lists.[33] Their careers varied wildly yet find one and you will find the others in the East India Company military service records. He was eighteen and his attention evidently wandered since *'as a mark of Courts displeasure at his conduct while at Chatham in copying his survey of a piece of land from the cadets of the [Royal Engineers] his contemporaries, he is to lose one step and to stand below Cadet Walker'*.[34] He wasn't alone in this punishment as Impey also incurred the *'Courts displeasure at his misconduct in copying certain surveys of land while at Chatham from those of 2 other Cadets'*.[35] George Francklin Atkinson's work was itself later copied, re-drawn and reproduced in a variety of medium from watercolours to woodcuts, line drawings to lithographs. The lithographic plates worked up by Day & Son have carried a wide variety of 'curry', the colouring varying enormously according to the taste of the publisher. Such methods of reproduction were the main means of copying original illustrations for publication during the 19th century – and he was clearly not immune to imitation himself. Losing a step meant loss of status in the Company's pecking order and could have serious implications for future progress in a system of promotion based entirely on seniority. As it turned out, Thomas Charles Phillpotts died on 7 September 1844 at Delhi and Reginald John Walker followed him on 24 April 1847 near Darjeeling.[36][37] Walker was Assistant Surveyor in the Great Trigonometrical Survey of India.[38] Though surveying seems like a comfortable job, miasmatic vapours and molestations of mosquitoes cursed those surveying swampland and exhaustion in the thin air of the Himalayas took its toll on even the fittest engineers. George Francklin Atkinson would soon be introduced to these privations and he was admitted to the services on 12 January 1842.[39]

He appeared in his new scarlet uniform resplendent with blue velvet facings and gold lace at Fort William, Calcutta on 7 July 1842. Ordered to do service with the sappers and miners at Delhi just over a week later, he had precious little time to acclimatise to new country and new clothes.[40] His father had returned from Afghanistan in January 1841 and was in residence as Superintending Surgeon in nearby Meerut. This salubrious station sat off the North East shoulder of Delhi and may well have been the inspiration for George Francklin Atkinson's barely fictional 'Kabob' in *Curry and Rice*. The town's *'obtrusively prepossessing'* aspect was only matched by the *'beauty and luxuriance of its gardens'*, and *'private Theatricals'* where *'the gallant votaries of Thespis get up for the amusement of delighted audiences melodramas of the most absorbing interest, and farces intensely facetious'*.[41] Clearly, more ink than blood was spilt in the European cantonments of the 1840s. If the whitewashed bungalows at Meerut insulated flagging English officers from oppressive Indian summers, the rest of the region was fully exposed to the white heat of the decade's four major wars. The Atkinson brothers played relatively minor roles in the Sind conquest, Gwalior campaigns and Sikh conflicts which spanned the period 1843–49, but take to the field they did. Frederick Dayot served with Sir Charles Napier in the Conquest of Sind in 1843 and his younger brother Charles D'Oyly manoeuvred with the 40th Native Infantry at Sagar. By the time of the Gwalior War in late 1843, Charles D'Oyly had been seconded to the Public Works Department and was *'in charge of the 14th or Saugar [Sagar] region'*.[42] A detachment such as this could be lucrative and leisurely and many officers saw extra-regimental postings as a key source of income and advancement. In his 1851 digest of military regulations, J H Stocqueler noted how *'in no service in the world are the pay and allowances upon so liberal a scale as in that of the East India Company.'* There were *'multitudinous instances and circumstances in which extra and additional allowances are granted'* and Charles D'Oyly was clearly turning his *'modicum of acquired knowledge to account'*.[43]

As a fully paid up *'Executive Engineer of the Allygurh [Aligarh] Division'* in June 1843, George Francklin Atkinson became involved in the construction and maintenance of a wide range of civil and military works.[44] Cantonments, forts, public works and edifices, roads, bridges, viaducts and canals were all articulating parts of a structure that flexed the sinews of war and tendons of trade. The laying of roads was pedestrian work but a necessary labour and one in which he found himself employed on 11 August 1843. Working as Assistant Engineer on the military road from Meerut to 'Umbailah' [Ambala] he helped survey, plan and construct the routes along which vital reinforcements would flow in 1857.[45] The roads were metalled with *'kunkur'* a carbonate deposit that dried rock hard in the sun and he was responsible for both raw materials and men. His relationship with the men in his command was complicated. There was clearly close observation (even down to the cow-hocked horse) as *'Troops of the Native Allies'* demonstrates and he was generally accurate in reproductions of equipment and clothing. He was capable of appreciation and appears affectionate to sporting men like *'Our Nuwab'* in *Curry and Rice*. His depictions of *'Sepoys at rifle practice'* could hardly be called grotesque and display intimate detail. We might detect pride in his description of the Sappers and Miners work on both sides at Delhi (see plate 18 of this volume, *Sappers at work in the batteries*). Yet his language is typically racist and his attitude to religion terribly insulting. *Curry and Rice* offers the thin excuse of satire to mediate its effects but all such pretence is lost with *The Campaign in India 1857–58*. He may have been giving his audience what they wanted to hear. Their enemy, trained and armed by the British as it was, had to be portrayed as a worthy opponent and a duplicitous foe. They were at once both *'stout mutineers'* and yet *'exceedingly bigoted'* (see plate 22 *Mutinous Sepoys*). This separation of physical ability from mental faculty was but one of the ingrained sectarian traits that the British increasingly displayed towards the people they ruled. It was not an attitude necessarily shared by the older generation of English moffusilites. James Atkinson was appreciative of the *'respectful antiquity'* of the region and conversant with Sanskrit, Persian and *'Hindoostanee'*.[46] He would surely have baulked at the final removal of Persian as the language of Government in 1837 and was happy to wear the decorations of a foreign power. The insignia of the third class Order of the Dooranee empire was presented to him by *'Shah Shooja-ool-Moolk, King of Affghanistan [who] hath been pleased to confer upon him, in testimony to His Majesty's approbation of the services, from time to time, rendered by him during the Campaign in Affghanistan'*.[47] Few such appellations or affectations could be expected to be entertained by the younger generation. As military rivals fell and evangelical missionary activity increased, there grew a feeling that *'the British had nothing to learn from India and much to teach it'*. A sense of *'imperial arrogance'* was quick to develop as the embers of the Gwalior and Sikh wars faded away.[48] Yet these victories were won at considerable loss of life to European and Native Infantry alike. Surgeon Robert James Atkinson served as a medical officer in the First Sikh War of 1845–46 and George Francklin Atkinson was *'placed at the disposal of Chief Engineer of the Army of Gwalior'* on 10th January 1844'.[49][50] Bloody as it was, the Gwalior War only lasted 48 hours and by the time he reached the field it was all over bar the shouting. He must have been detached for a particular task as he was back on the roads two months later. This time he was indisposed to the *'Supt. Engineer North Western Provinces'*, again for employment *'on the new line of artillery road from Meerut to Umballa [Ambala]*' on 14 March 1844.[51]

If all this sounds like the kind of exploits a senior officer might be expected to undertake, it should be remembered that he was still a 2nd Lieutenant and only 22 years old. Despite his extra duties, pay and privileges, he was still on the bottom rung of the ladder and earning a mere 192 *rupees*, 18 *annas* and 6 *paise* a month.[52] The demise of Thomas Charles Phillpotts in September at Delhi, finally meant promotion to 1st Lieutenant in the Bengal Engineers on 30 November 1844.[53][54] His pay increased to 234 *rupees* and 14 *annas* but as he was a still a relatively junior officer, his vital *'tent allowance'* was still only 50 rupees a month.[55] A certain amount of envy at the *'expanse of canvas and extent of ground occupied'* may be detected in his description of *'A scene in camp'* (see plate 4) and the size of a man's tent seems an obvious way in which status could be marked out in the lines. If promotion came slowly, sickness came swiftly to those pioneers who cut roads through jungle, swamp and plain. A furlough (leave of absence) would normally only be granted after ten years service in India but a sick certificate could be a ticket back to *'the balmy air of an English winters day'*.[56] He was *'granted a furlo to Europe on S.C.'* (sick certificate) on 30

January 1846 and left India for England on 9 February.[57] Three years seemed plenty of time to recuperate and he described how on *'returning from the East to a more temperate clime, in search of health, and anxious to visit a portion of Europe comparatively little trodden, I was induced to direct my steps to the North'.*[58] The rest of the family remained in the East. James Atkinson was ready to retire and direct his solicitors on the finer points of his will, Robert James Atkinson was newly married and Frederick Dayot Atkinson was a career climbing infantry officer.[59][60] Charles D'Oyly Atkinson would have little time to savour the *'private letters, penned on the spot for friends at home'* that formed the basis for his first book *Pictures from the North in pen and pencil* as he died at sea on 15 October 1848 at the age of 27.[61]

George Francklin Atkinson was presented to the Court of Queen Victoria on 24 February 1847 by the Earl of Limerick *'on his return from India'.*[62] What better way to reintroduce yourself to London society than to appear at a Royal levee? This social occasion set the tone for his furlough and he did not convalesce quietly. He travelled across large parts of Northern Europe and produced *Pictures from the North in pen and pencil* in 1848. The cooler climate was supposedly conducive to the suppression of malaria but over exertion seems to have worsened his condition. It was whilst playing cards in St Petersburg that his illness showed its hand and he folded.

'For my part I was unable to see it out, for two exceedingly disagreeable friends caused me to decamp - fever and ague: two very insinuating Oriental visitors, who tyrannically brought me to Europe, and who are perpetually intruding on my quietude with their parasitical attentions. In the plains of Hindostan duty compelled me to be a dweller of tents during the very hottest season of the year, when with the combined delights of a thermometer at 120°, a grilling sun, and a scorching hot wind, followed by heavy rains, a jungle, flooded and swampy, with the miasmatic influences of noxious vegetation in a state of decay, it is not astonishing that they made their appearance. The heat of a canvass abode, under the burning rays of a tropical sun, is no joke I can assure the reader who may be sitting "snug at home at ease". Imagine our device to keep the head cool, which is by investing it with a towel well-saturated with water, and which becomes dry as chalk in ten minutes if not re-wetted. The heat however is bearable and even healthy. It is the damp and insalubrious vapours that engender fever and ague. A Russian Esculapius, with a bleak countenance of awful longitude, is called in, and repels the intruders with his remedial abominations, which to prevent a relapse are as bad as the attack itself. Quinine! pah! one's head oscillates at the very remembrance, and to have to quaff bumpers periodically throughout the day, and in "night gown and slippers" to vegetate on tea and broth, feeling all the while so ravenous that the sunny side of a donkey would be an absolute trifle to demolish'.[63]

Pictures from the North was reviewed by *The Literary Examiner* on Saturday 9 September 1848 (issue 2119). It concluded that *'the book has no pretension but that which it fairly fulfils'* faint praise that neither provoked nor condemned. It was not a heavyweight piece of travel writing yet would *'entertain an idle hour very pleasantly... is pictorial, sunny and genial; with masked balls, reviews, polkas, mazourkas and theatres; peasantry and parades, steam boats, billiards and boulevards'*. Ultimately the reviewer sidesteps responsibility for passing judgement and when *'we have appended a few brief extracts, the reader will be able to judge for himself of the amount of entertainment in the book'*. His sketches *'in themselves characteristic'* were *'very cleverly transferred to wood'* for reproduction. The impression gained is of an indifferent reviewer rather than a terrible book. This first volume clearly provided a pattern for his later work. Just as *Pictures from the North* recorded and ridiculed European society, *Curry and Rice* satirised and serialised the English in India. As his furlough came to a close, the next chapter of his career commenced at Calcutta on 5 February 1849.[64]

On returning to duty he reported at Fort William in Calcutta. Here he was appointed *'Executive Engineer of the 14th or Saugor [Sagar] division'*, the last post of his brother Charles D'Oyly Atkinson.[65] This is quite touching and we might presume that he returned to the region to support the widowed Harriet Maria Atkinson and her 9-year-old daughter Jane Harriet Atkinson. The Bengal Military Fund provided a widow's pension (for subscribers), but at a third of her husband's salary they could well have struggled. The extended circle of the family was presumably the main source of sustenance. Frederick Dayot and James Augustus Atkinson as partners in the Delhi and London Bank Ltd, would one day be able to offer more financial support than the majority of bereaved families.[66]

The loss of his brother tilted George Francklin's axis away from the Delhi circle and into the orbit of Benares [Varanasi] in January 1850. This new orientation brought him into contact with a new set of people and it may have been here, whilst working as *'Executive Engineer of the 5th or Benares division'*, that he proposed to Catherine Ellen O'Dowda.[67] The two were married on 1 July 1850 at St Paul's Cathedral in Calcutta and their daughter Eva C Atkinson was born at *'Ghazeepoire'* [Gazipur] on 3 October 1851.[68] Female voices were rarely recorded and information on daughters is scarce compared to military men in Victorian

Figure 1 George Francklin Atkinson and assistants surveying swampland in the 1840s (Atkinson 1848). *Courtesy of The British Library*

society. In contrast, the views of their eldest son Ernest George Atkinson find easy expression in the large amount of historical synthesis he published at the Public Record Office in London. As he is described as 'the eldest son of Captain George Francklin Atkinson' in his *Times* marriage announcement, we might assume there was more progeny, but details have thus far proved elusive.[69]

As the world turned and Eva C Atkinson woke under an Indian sun, her grandfather James Atkinson stepped into the long shadows of a late English summer. His literally apoplectic death marked a stuttering end to 42 years of service in India. Fluent in at least four languages, his last moments were punctuated by a fit of apoplexy in his residence at 18 Dorset Square, Marylebone on 7 August 1852.[70] George Francklin Atkinson had spent ten years in service and was only now '*reported to have acquired a competent knowledge of Hindoostanee*'.[71] James was interred in Brompton Cemetery which in Victorian London was very much the place to be seen dead in. Charles D'Oyly Atkinson was laid to rest here four years earlier and it seems likely they shared a family plot. Furlough could be granted for '*urgent private affairs*' but families in India must have become used to the sudden loss and quick burial of family and friends.[72] Although it is not mentioned in his service papers, it seems natural (and perfectly possible) that George Francklin would have tried to return to England for his father's funeral. Events intervened to ensure he never made it to London as the Second Anglo-Burmese War erupted in late 1852. His role in this conflict is known through the work of Sidney Henry Jones Parry and no reference to his Burmese service is given in his records at the British Library. Parry's book *An Old Soldier's Memories* pencils in George Francklin as principal scene-painter for theatricals given *'to enliven and cheer up the men'.*[73] If Parry fumbles his lines over names, ranks and dates, his memory of Atkinson is clear enough.

'Luckily the fleet had canvas galore, and still more luckily we had Atkinson of the Bengal Engineers, who was a host in himself with pencil and brush. Reader, have you ever seen Curry and Rice? If not, get it, and you will be well repaid your trouble. You will see what we had in our principal scene-painter. Glover of the 51ˢᵗ K.O.L.I., and I washed in sky, etc., and Glover filled in other parts, for he was a fair draughtsman, and then Atkinson finished off, leaving tableaux that were the admiration of all beholders.[74]

Atkinson was presumably engaged in military engineering throughout this campaign yet, as with the actions of 1857, what people most remembered was his artistry. His artwork often occupies centre stage in the English drama of the 'mutiny' while his public works are relegated to the wings. Yet it is these buildings and roads that are still lived with by people in present day Haryana and Uttar Pradesh. We would do well to remember this when considering his more unusual work. The Benares College, designed and built by Major Kittoe of the Bengal Engineers in 1833, was patronised by Lieutenant-Governor James Thomason and embellished by several archaeological fragments from nearby sites. When the Lieutenant-Governor died in 1853, a massive monolith bound for the College gardens naturally acquired the title 'Thomason's Pillar'. *Allens Indian Mail* for Friday 28 July 1854 was able to report that *the Thomason Pillar is, at last, standing erect in the college garden* and gave *'all honour to Captain Atkinson, the ex-engineer!'*.[75] Atkinson was involved in the colonial attitude of appropriating the past to justify the present but in doing so, he recovered monuments the type of which would later become rallying points for the rise of Indian nationalism.

Another appointment and another move took George Francklin Atkinson away from Benares [Varanasi] and back to the *'Umballa Division of the North West Provinces'* on 30 May 1854.[76] After 12 years of service he might have expected promotion to Captain and a pay rise to be imminent. He was confirmed in one expectation and confounded in the other when he was promoted Brevet-Captain. This meant he could claim the *rank* but not the *pay* of his new position. Frustrating though this undoubtedly was, the final retirement of his predecessor was the only obstacle in his path and he became full Captain on 19 November 1855.[77] He was promoted ahead of administrative changes in the Public Works Department. This is important as it provides some of the best evidence for his location during the early stages of the crisis in 1857. The 'Umballah Division' of public works was to be divided between *'works in the hills'* (Upper Umballah Division) and *'works in the plains'* (Lower Umballah Division). As executive engineer of the Upper Division he was responsible for all military and public works from Ambala itself up into the rarefied air of the hill stations at Kasauli, Sabathu and Dagshai.[78] It is therefore likely that he was at least in Ambala if not North of it when events began to unfold in the first half of 1857. The cool air of the hill stations was supposed to take the heat out of European constitutions yet even here some soldiers were prone to overheating. Her Majesty's 98th Regiment of Foot seem to have objected to their barracks at Dagshai as Captain Atkinson brought forward a claim of £131.4s.1d. against them on 10 September 1856. Whatever their cause, his delay in bringing forward the claim for was *'not considered satisfactory'* by the Public Works department. They were clearly not impressed by this lazy accounting and his promotion to '1st Captain' was cancelled on 14 December 1856.[79] His position may not have been helped by the satirical and sometimes scandalous sketches he began to produce as editor of *The Delhi Sketchbook* in 1855. Known as *'the Indian Punch'* it contained many prototype characters later portrayed in *Curry and rice*.[80] His sketch of *'How our Sporting Griff tries his luck at tandem'* for the 1 September edition was the obvious inspiration for 'Our Sporting Griff' in *Curry and Rice*. This was harmless enough, but unflattering works such as *'Heroes of the Nineteenth Century 100 Miles from the Camp of Exercise'* for the 1 January 1855 may have been too close to the bone for some senior officers.[81]

The roads that George Francklin Atkinson laid literally paved the way for the advance of the Delhi Field Force out of the hill stations and down towards Ambala in 1857.[82] They saved the soles of many a soldier but it was a rather different soul his latest and greatest edifice was concerned with. Seventeen new church spires scaled the heavens in the Punjab Territories between 1856 and 1858. They were built at the skyhigh cost of *'3½ lakhs of Rupees or £35,000'* and provided accommodation for 8,000 Christian souls.[83] This was a vast amount of money and equivalent to over 60 million pounds of the United Kingdom's Gross Domestic Product in 2006.[84] How much of that made its way into the pockets of the Indian masons, carpenters, glaziers and labourers who actually constructed them is not clear. Some materials and expertise may have been imported, but the lions share of this work must have gone to the local builders. His contribution to this evangelical effort came in the form of St Paul's in Ambala.

'Of these churches during the past two years progress has been made with the Umballa church, which is complete, with the exception of the tower. It is a fine structure of the decorated gothic style, and does great credit to the architectural taste of the Executive Engineer, Captain G.F. Atkinson. During the crisis the enclosure of the church was fortified, and the building itself was prepared as a rendezvous for European

residents in the event of attack. No attack however was made, and the beautiful church has not been in any way defaced.'[85]

This *'beautiful church'* surely did as much credit to the largely non-Christian workforce that actually built it, men who probably did not understand the symbolism of the architecture they were contracted to construct. If they did not have a firm grasp of the finer points of ecclesiastical architecture, they would undoubtedly have understood the impression an imported image of nave and chancel could imprint upon India. Missionary influence was generally seen as malign and no wonder when temple lands (of any denomination) were confiscated and holy buildings driven through by Company roads.[86]

Although he was hardly a religious zealot like the evangelical, energetic and utterly exhausting Reverend Midgely John Jennings (the Chaplain of Delhi), Atkinson shared in the general attitude of Christian belief that the Empire was divinely ordained. His attitude to missionaries was gently mocking and aspects of men like the Reverend Doctor Procknow (the enterprising principal of the Berlin Missionary Institution entrenched at Koteghur) may well be seen in the carefully contrived plate 'Our German Missionary' in *Curry and Rice*. He seems to have approved of *'Our Padre'* who entertained religious views of *'the broad and popular kind'* and was *'unctuous in appearance, redolent of fat, and with a face beaming like the sun on a gravel-walk'.*[87] The engineers were encouraged to demonstrate a *'propriety of architectural style'* and *'endeavour has been made to erect buildings, which, while fulfilling the requirements of an Eastern climate, may yet present an exterior indicating their sacred character and preserve the religious associations so much venerated in the mother country'.*[88] His church was appreciated as a *'good specimen of the decorated gothic'*, a splendid revival of the early English style dating from the late 13th to early 14th century.[89] A large knave was flanked by vaulted aisles with circular windows illuminating the brick built body of the building. The tower was four square, perpendicular and decorated with finials. His taste in the Gothic revival cuts through the satire of *Curry and Rice* with some acidity.

'There, that square whitewashed edifice, with an excrescence at one end, looking for all the world like an extinguisher on a three-dozen chest! - what is it? You may well ask. It is the church! A regular Protestant building! Protesting against everything architectural, aesthetic, ornamental, or useful; designed and built according to a Government prescription'.[90]

The church illustrated in *Our Station* bears more than a passing resemblance to St John's in Meerut and it seems to be the target for his attack. His own creation would be targeted twice in the years to come. St Paul's offered safe refuge to European refugees in May 1857 when Major General George Anson ordered the church to be entrenched *'for the protection of the inhabitants when the troops move'.*[91] It was eventually garrisoned by at least 500 sick English soldiers bolstered by horse artillery, light cavalry and native infantry. Today St Paul's flying buttresses stand out like skeletal collarbones as it bakes in the sun and soaks in the rain. It fell victim to fighter-bombers in the India-Pakistan war of 1965 and only the shell remains.

His church was much admired and we might well see his hand in others of the region. The routine military works of an engineer officer however, were more concerned with the lords temporal than spiritual. He followed Sir Charles Napier's plans of barracks for European troops in the hill stations and expanded on them in the Artillery Mess House at Meerut.[92] As Captain Atkinson's buildings ministered to both body and soul of the European soldiery, Major Frederick Dayot Atkinson administered the army as Deputy to the Military Secretary of the Government of India.[93] Robert James Atkinson was on furlough to England and the youngest brother James Augustus Atkinson was about to begin his ministry as rector of Hollinwood in Oldham.[94] As 1856 came to an end, Captain Atkinson's future must have appeared lined with an endless conurbation of barracks and bungalows, cantonments and churches.

The *Bengal Service Army Lists* at the British Library are the main source of information for British officers of the East India Company army. It is therefore extremely frustrating that a large blank space marks out George Francklin Atkinson's Bengal Service Army record for 1857. His contemporaries Archibald Impey and James Pattle Beadle are both mentioned on a large double page spread for the Chatham graduates of 1842. Impey's entry is extensive and details his calling to the field force *'to repel the... mutineers from Oude'* yet for Atkinson, answer came there none.[95] As a fully trained engineer, his skills would be of vital importance to the Delhi Field Force. True enough, his time in India was almost exclusively spent in construction not demolition, but officers of experience could not be spared and each was employed to the best of their abilities. So why does he fail to appear to any great significance in the English accounts of Delhi? And why did he not detail the exploits of his fellow Bengal Engineers in the bloody destruction of the Kashmiri Gate? In his foreword to David Blomfield's edition of *Lahore to Lucknow; The Indian Mutiny Journal of Arthur Moffat Lang*, Lieutenant General Sir Derek Lang describes how *'Atkinson did not serve at Delhi himself, but he was able to sketch the soldiers from life, along with their weapons and beasts of burden. It seems that he gathered the rest of his material from his fellow officers'.*[96] If this is the case then it begs the question where was he in 1857 and what was he doing?

We know his health was not good. Malaria manifested itself several times throughout his career in India and it may well have kept him from marching on Delhi. By April 1858 he was ready to return to Europe on another sick certificate for a 15-month furlough.[97] It seems the old trouble kept advancing upon him and no matter how much road he lay down as perpetual executive engineer of 'Upper Umballah [Ambala]', it was an illness he could not outrun.[98] Perhaps the best evidence for his general location comes in his final, brilliant and barely known work of 1859 *Indian Spices for English Tables*.[99] That it is rarely seen is not surprising as it seems to have had an extremely limited print run. Manuscript notes on the inside cover of The British Library's copy indicate that it was personally '*presented to the Library India Office by Rev. Canon J.A. Atkinson, brother of the author*' and is signed by him.[100] Worthy of a full reprint in itself, Atkinson makes himself the final target for his satire in Plate XXVII of *Indian Spices* here reproduced as figure 2.

Figure 2 Plate XXVII from Indian Spices for English Tables (Atkinson 1860).
Courtesy of The British Library

No portrait is known to survive of George Francklin Atkinson, but who would want one when his character lives through his caricature? His 'self-portrait' as he '*hastes to the battlefield and views (from afar) the smoke and terrible din, and prepares in his mind a comprehensive report for our column*' is revelatory as it clearly shows how far removed he was from the chaotic siege lines at Delhi and that he knew himself to be so. Some of his information may well have been derived from the '*party of knowing ones who have congregated to discuss scandal*' in the coffee shop where he '*furnishes a little diversion*' rather than plunging headlong into the fray. He acknowledges the popular appeal of his work and the formula to which it was written as he rushes to his tent and scribbles '*a vivid narrative of the action leaving hiatus etc for the subsequent insertion of names of the glorious fallen and the glorious living. The narrative is read throughout Europe with a crushing and thrilling interest*'. *The Morning Chronicle* went into panegyrics when reviewing *The Campaign in India*.

In the illustration of the proceedings which terminated in a result almost as miraculous as that of the fall of the walls of Jericho before the blast of trumpets, Captain Atkinson has in this elegant volume applied his facile and graphic powers of sketching [and a] faithful pictorial record of the principal scenes and incidents which took place during this stirring and tremendous campaign, can scarcely fail to meet with a ready and cordial welcome among Englishmen, and such a record we have in "The Campaign in India".[101]

It concluded that the book was *'a most valuable and interesting record of the greatest event in the military history of the civilized world'*, a conclusion we may well dispute today and which even then must have left those who recently served in the Crimea feeling somewhat overlooked.[102]

As executive engineer in charge of works in the hills above Ambala and unable to follow the field force due to malaria, we might be safe in assuming that he never made it down to Delhi. We do know that officers with similar conditions still managed to do very hard work in the siege (Captain W S R Hodson for one) and that cholera, dysentery and 'wastage' were a constant threat to front line troops. Yet it appears Atkinson had a further reason to remain. He was ordered to. Greatly concerned for the plight of refugees who were already beginning to trickle back to the hill stations and the women and children sent from Ambala to the safety of the hills, Major General George Anson *'sent directions to Captain Atkinson to do whatever was necessary for the protection of Kasauli on 16 May 1857'*.[103]

At Kasauli *'some slight defences had been erected and the verandahs of the barracks were barricaded, and supplies laid in'* (see plate 26). This seems to be the kind of work he was employed in for the majority of the crisis. He was not a front line engineer and was given responsibility for maintaining vital 'back areas' and ensuring refugees were looked after. Perhaps one of the reasons that elephants, bullock carts, palanquins, camel trains and mail carts receive so much attention from Atkinson is that they were literally passing him by. Having said that, he would not have struggled for sources. Wounded soldiers and displaced families kept him in touch with proceedings. Letters and notes from friends at the front flowed up Atkinson's arterial roads and into *The Campaign in India*. It may seem curious that the Bengal Engineers do not figure large in his description of it, but this may simply reflect the fact that so many of this *'zealous, indefatigable body of young officers'* (see plate 18 *Sappers at work in the batteries*) died during the assault. Not that their story would remain untold for long. News of Lieutenants Salkeld and Home's subsequent decoration with the Victoria Cross spread fast and their tale would be told in triplicate elsewhere. Atkinson had plenty to write about and some of his illustrations seem to have been worked up to order as the following extract from Hodson's letters shows.

'June 23rd - An amusing story is told à propos of the fight this morning. A rascally Pandy, thinking all was over, put his head out of the window of one of the houses, in the shade of which a few Europeans and Goorkhas were resting. One of the latter jumped up, laid hold of the rebel by his hair, and with one chop of his 'kookrie' took off his head. Atkinson should make a sketch of this for the Illustrated News'.[104]

Within seven days Brigadier Showers (commanding the 2nd Fusiliers on the ridge before Delhi) had received *'a very clever sketch, from Atkinson'* of this very incident in which *'all the faces are inimitably portrayed'*.[105] News travelled fast between Delhi and the hill stations and it is perhaps significant that the letters written by Brevet-Major O H S G Anson to his wife in Kasauli note the days that the mail *dâk* didn't turn up at Delhi rather than the times it did. It took slightly longer for his sketch to reach the English press and *Incidents in the camp - prompt execution of a treacherous mutineer* appeared in the *Illustrated London News* on 10 October 1857. The 'correspondent of the artist' quoted in the accompanying text may well have been Hodson himself.[106] The sketch is described as *'a ludicrous, though a tragic scene'* and is further captioned *Tragical adventure in the Subseemundee* [Sabzi Mandi - the vegetable market].[107] By the time *The Campaign in India* was published, he had obviously decided that the loss of one's head was more incidental than tragic and re-titled his illustration *Incident at the Subzee Mundee* (plate 12). *Tragical adventures in the vegetable market* doesn't quite have the same ring. Atkinson places a comic twist, perhaps only amusing to victorious English officers in 1857, on events that to the population of Delhi were little short of daylight robbery and frequently murderous. His depiction of *Prize Agents extracting treasure* (plate 23) illustrates an event that found much currency in gossip and accounts after the fall of the city. If locking your victim in a darkened cell and firing pistol shots over his head failed to elicit the correct response, a pistol bullet actually fired through the turban could have the desired effect.[108] Looting was supposed to be illegal and Prize Agents were employed to police plundered goods and divide the proceeds of sale among soldiers. This rarely happened in an equitable manner. Robbery was seen as just reward for *'the many weeks of privation, danger, and death that they were exposed to ere the city fell into their possession'* (plate 23). Where Prize Agents did get in on the act, their methods were sometimes far from humane.

Atkinson's description of the capture and death of the King of Delhi's sons by Captain W S R Hodson on 22 September 1857, justifies their murder on the grounds that they had *'directed and witnessed the butchery of unoffending [European] women and children'*. His illustration *Capture and Death of the Shahzadahs* (plate 24) clothes the three princes in an air of relative respectability as they are shot by Hodson and we should remember that Atkinson dedicates his book to 'Her Most Gracious Majesty the

Queen'. Regicide was understandably a touchy subject. In reality, it seems that Hodson forced Mirza Mughal, Khizr Sultan and Abu Bakr to strip before shooting them in the chest at very close range with a Colt revolver. He then stole their signet rings, decorated *tulwars* (swords) and *bazubands* (armlets).[109] British victory, ironically achieved with an army more Indian than English, was seen as *'the blessing of Almighty God'*, divine intervention against diabolical cruelty that *'strove to destroy every European and Christian in the land'* (see introduction, this volume). Time and again, atrocity was clothed in religious terms, which find parallels today in both East and West.

George Francklin Atkinson is frequently cited as a correspondent for the *Illustrated London News*. The first identifiable instance of his work comes in a series of sketches made during the First Sikh War and published two days after he left India for England on sick certificate on 7 February 1846. He would no doubt be familiar with the Sikh *khalsa* and his illustrations show a degree of detail, yet his role in that particular conflict remains obsure. Short of a front line despatch from the man himself, it seems likely that he remained employed on the road from Meerut to Ambala, an essential route for Sir Hugh Gough's train of artillery. When he describes himself as a 'special correspondent', he may well have been mocking the tendency of anyone with intelligence on the events in India to offer them up as Gospel truth as soon as heard. Although *'Irregular Cavalry of the Bengal Army'* didn't make it into his book, *'Pushing Forward British Troops to Delhi'* certainly did and appears as *'Reinforcements Proceeding to Delhi'* in plate 10 of this volume. His *'Interior of a Subaltern's tent before Delhi'* also made it into *The Campaign in India* but the *Illustrated London News* version is far more elegantly drawn than the tinted lithograph of the book itself. This is really the difficulty in identifying Atkinson's work in the popular press as it was so often re-drawn. He may well have provided copy for earlier issues of the *Illustrated London News* but, unsigned and unattributed, we have to rely on content and composition. If we cannot compare them to published examples, we cannot be sure that he ever contributed anything more than is readily comparable in known cases. His publishers W Thacker and Co. claim *'his drawings of Indian life and scenery often appeared in the Illustrated London News'* but there seems scant evidence of them for much of the 1850s.[110]

Whatever his exact role in the events of 1857–58, his family appear to have made it through unscathed. Robert James Atkinson responded to an order recalling officers to India on 6 July 1857 and was *'appointed to the Medical Charge of Troops for Calcutta to be embarked on the ship "Octavia" about the 25th inst.'*.[111] Frederick Dayot Atkinson had the morbid task of collecting casualty returns from field officers and must have recognised several names from his old regiment as the lists rolled across his desk. George Francklin Atkinson's recall to the old job of 'executive engineer Public Works, Upper Sirhind' must have been more than flesh could bear and he quickly obtained three months leave to Bombay commencing on 20 September 1858.[112] This was described as a *'preparatory to furlo'*, a period of leave to ready him for *another* period of leave. He was clearly not well and his furlough to Europe on sick certificate was actually brought forward to 30 April 1858.[113] That the Company let him go at a time when the crisis was far from over, may well be an indication of the extent of his illness. If nothing else, it finally afforded time to polish off and publish both *Curry and Rice: On Forty Plates* and *The Campaign in India 1857–58*.

The Campaign in India was first advertised in *The Times* on 30 October 1858. The publishers promised it would be available *'before mid-December'* and *'in the hands of subscribers by Christmas'*. *Curry and Rice* appeared alongside it in *The Times* on 2nd November and was finally published on 10 December 1858.[114] The *Morning Chronicle* picked up *Curry and Rice* on Wednesday 15 December 1858 and panned it to within an inch of its life. It described Atkinson's preface as *'a mere jumble of fine words, the very balderdash of balderdash'* and counselled the reader *'not to measure the merits of the sketches themselves by the opinion he may form of the quality of the preface, if he be disposed to give the author his due; for it is justice to say that the caviare which is served up as an introduction to "Curry and Rice" is decidedly the worst course of all'*. Although it was happy to concede that *'Captain George Francklin Atkinson is, no doubt, a most jovial, straightforward, go-happy, well-met sort of a man, who would not say an unkind thing if he could help it'*, this was precisely the reason why *'his forty "plates" lack the quantity of curry requisite for so much rice'*. His coloured lithographs were the books' saving grace and they were *'much the better part of Capt. Atkinson's work'*.[115]

'The book, which is elegantly got up and well printed is dedicated to Mr Thackeray, but we cannot possibly see how that gentleman's permissions to allow Captain Atkinson's 'little craft' to get 'under his lee' can possibly save it from a just criticism. The "howling gusts of criticism" and "lashing waves from reviewers" as the author expresses it are not usually lavished on so inoffensive a "bear".[116]

William Makepeace Thackeray's letter thanking Atkinson for his dedication was actually published in full by W Thacker and Company. Writing from the Hotel Bristol, Place Vendome on 27 December 1857, Thackeray wrote how he received his *'beautiful book'* in London and that:

'It was very interesting to me to see what my native country is like now. I have far-off visions of great saloons and people dancing in them, enormous idols and fireworks, rides on elephants or in jigs, and fogs clearing away and pagodas appearing over the trees, yellow rivers and budgerows etc. I'm always interested about the place and your sketches came to me as very welcome, besides being exceedingly pretty, cheerful, and lively. I hope the book will succeed. It must have been an awful bill to pay'.[117]

It was a good job he didn't send him *The Campaign in India* as he might have got a very different impression! Thackeray's cousin Edward Talbot Thackeray was a 2nd Lieutenant in the Bengal Engineers and won the Victoria Cross at Delhi on 16 September 1857.[118] Atkinson was clearly making the most of his Indian connections but even Thackeray did not think that his name would deter the *'awful and inscrutable'* editors of *The Times* from attacking *Curry and rice*.[119] Perhaps the fairest comment made about the book at the time came from *The Calcutta Review* when it said *'it is we know fearfully abused, which is not a bad criterion of the faithfulness of its portraiture'*.[120] Sadly, Captain George Francklin Atkinson would not have read his final review. He died at Bellevue near Paris on 15 December 1859.

His death was reported in the *Belfast News Letter* on Friday 30 December and reached the *Friend of India* on Thursday 2 February 1860. Few details were given but it seems he had finally succumbed to his long-standing illness. He was 37. His work outlived him and prospers in multiple volumes on the events of 1857 in India. Atkinson's plates are often reproduced piecemeal and without the accompanying text. This volume, reproducing *The Campaign in India; 1857–58* for the first time, unites text and illustrations and places them in the order that George Francklin Atkinson intended them to be read. In providing this context we remain fully aware of the prejudice and predilections displayed therein. The voices of ordinary Delhiwallahs, sepoys and havildars are barely heard yet the plates are endearing and enduring. They encapsulate the English experience of the crisis and their response to it. Hinduism, Sikhism and Islam are entirely sidelined in favour of a Christian ideology tailored to the dominance of Empire. His expressions are the language of an English elite denigrating their enemies in the terms they knew would provoke the most insult. Yet if you were looking for a record of the attitudes of the English in India during 1857 you could do far worse than read George Francklin Atkinson's *The Campaign in India; 1857-58.*

Notes

[1]   Boase 1965
[2]   Matthew & Harrison 2004
[3]   See entry for James Atkinson in the India Office Records Biographical File at the British Library and Matthew & Harrison 2004.
[4]   Matthew & Harrison 2004 and L/MIL/9/390/365 entry for Robert James Atkinson in the Assistant Surgeons, Surgeons and the Indian Medical Service papers at the British Library.
[5]   See India Office Records Biographical File and L/MIL/9/390/365 for Robert James Atkinson; see Matthew & Harrison 2004 and N/1/9/268 for James Atkinson's marriage to Jane Bathie in the Bengal baptisms, marriages and burials at the British Library. James Atkinson is certainly the father of Robert James Atkinson.
[6]   For Frederick Dayot Atkinson see N/1/10/96; for Charles D'Oyly Atkinson see N/1/11/88 and L/MIL/9/179/374-80 in the Cadet Papers at the British Library.
[7]   Matthew & Harrison 2004
[8]   See Misc. Notices in The Quarterly Oriental Magazine Review and Register Vol. IV. Nos. VII and VIII July - December 1825: clxxxi. (Thacker and Co., London).
[9]   Sneyd ND
[10] Ward 1996: 251
[11] Burke 1848:100; David 2002: 67
[12] David 2002; Ward 1996; Hibbert 1983: 415
[13] Crawford 1914
[14] L/MIL/9/177/369-77, Cadet Papers, British Library.
[15] L/MIL/9/179/374-80, Cadet Papers, British Library.
[16] Stocqueler 1851: 276
[17] See L/MIL/9/189/158-63, Cadet Papers, British Library. The school presumably provided a preparatory education in an atmosphere of propriety.
[18] See L/MIL/9/177/369-77 for Frederick Dayot Atkinson and L/MIL/9/179/374-80 for Charles D'Oyly Atkinson, both in the Cadet Papers series at the British Library.

[19] Crawford 1914

[20] East India Register 1845: 91

[21] See N/1/54/92, Bengal baptisms, marriages and burials, British Library.

[22] See N/1/56/160, Bengal baptisms, marriages and burials, British Library.

[23] D'Oyly 1825: 182

[24] Atkinson 1858

[25] Stocqueler 1851: 278-9

[26] Atkinson 1842: 70-1

[27] L/MIL/10/34/11, Bengal Service Army Lists, British Library.

[28] United Service Journal 1840: 417

[29] Atkinson 1842:178

[30] United Service Journal 1840: 418-20

[31] L/MIL/10/45/436, Bengal Service Army Lists, British Library.

[32] *London Gazette* no. 19937 for 5 Jan. 1841 and Bengal Service Army Lists at L/MIL/10/34/11, British Library.

[33] After 1843 the Bengal Service Army Lists provide identification numbers for each officer (or groups of officers), which remain the same in subsequent volumes to 1858. See L/MIL/10/20-69 at the British Library.

[34] L/MIL/10/34/11, Bengal Service Army Lists, British Library.

[35] L/MIL/10/34/9, Bengal Service Army Lists, British Library.

[36] Urban 1844

[37] L/MIL/10/41/436, Bengal Service Army Lists, British Library.

[38] Urban 1848: 22

[39] L/MIL/10/34/11, Bengal Service Army Lists, British Library.

[40] L/MIL/10/34/11, Bengal Service Army Lists, British Library.

[41] Atkinson 1858: pls 2, 37, 30

[42] East India Register 1845: 50

[43] Stocqueler 1851: 284, 276

[44] L/MIL/10/34/11, Bengal Service Army Lists, British Library.

[45] East India Register 1845: 50

[46] Atkinson 1842: xi

[47] Bulletins and other State Intelligence 1841: 796

[48] Dalrymple 2006: 70

[49] Crawford 1914

[50] L/MIL/10/34/11, Bengal Service Army Lists, British Library.

[51] L/MIL/10/37/436, Bengal Service Army Lists, British Library.

[52] Stocqueler 1851: 286

[53] Urban 1844

[54] L/MIL/10/41/436, Bengal Service Army Lists, British Library.

[55] Stocqueler 1851: 286

[56] Atkinson 1858: pl. 40

[57] L/MIL/10/41/436, Bengal Service Army Lists, British Library.

[58] Atkinson 1848: v

[59] Robert James Atkinson, married Ellen Brett, daughter of John Brett Esq. 'of the Old Kent Road' at the Cathedral Church in Calcutta on 2 February 1846 (Burke 1846)

[60] See Atkinson 1848: iii. and India Office Family History search results for Charles D'Oyly Atkinson on the British Library website at www.http://indiafamily.bl.uk/UI/. Charles D'Oyly Atkinson composed his will in the presence of his older brother Frederick Dayot Atkinson on 29 September 1848. The voyage (presumably back to England) obviously proved too much for him. His wife Harriet Maria Atkinson was the sole executrix and beneficiary of the will and it was proved at London on 12 January 1849. See PROB/11/2086 at the National Archives.

[61] L/MIL/10/48/436, Bengal Service Army Lists, British Library.

[62] Burke 1846: 373

[63] Atkinson 1848: 119-20

[64] L/MIL/10/48/436, Bengal Service Army Lists, British Library.

[65] See Supplement to the *London Gazette* 25 February 1869 p. 1332.

[66] L/MIL/10/50/436, Bengal Service Army Lists, British Library.

[67] See *The Times* 1 July 1850 for the Atkinson's marriage announcement and the 1851 Bengal and Agra

Directory (S Smith and Co.) for the birth of their daughter.

[68] See *The Times* for 30 January 1892.

[69] Matthew & Harrison 2004 and *Medical Times and Gazette* 1852, New Series, Vol. The Fifth, Old Series - Vol. XXVI p. 179.

[70] L/MIL/10/51/436 section dated August 1851, Bengal Service Army Lists, British Library.

[71] L/MIL/10/58/436, Bengal Service Army Lists, British Library.

[72] Stocqueler 1851: 289

[73] Parry 1897: 47

[74] Parry 1897: 42

[75] Allens Indian Mail Vol. XII, no. 249: 9

[76] Allens India Mail Vol. XIV Jan-Dec. 1856 (Allen & Co. London): 162. The sources are a little confusing as to the exact order of promotion as the appointments are invariably post dated.

[77] *Allens India Mail* Vol. XIV Jan-Dec. 1856 p. 705.

[78] See Bengal Service Army Lists, L/MIL/10/62/436, British Library. Two hundred years later in 2006 this amount of money equates to £8, 161.34 (retail price index), £12, 399.46 (gross domestic product deflater), £79, 600.65 (average earnings index), £102, 666.04 (per capita gross domestic product) or £221, 865.83 (basic gross domestic product). Derived from calculators and data sets at http://www.measuringworth.com

[79] See advertisement for W Thacker and Co., London, as it appears in the end pages of Poole 1912 .

[80] Atkinson 1855. Series exists as bound volume 1850–57 at the British Library.

[81] It was two-way traffic along these arterial routes. They were vital for the reinforcement of both the Delhi field force and the sepoy army flocking to the city itself.

[82] Derived from data sets and calculators at http//:www.measuringworth.com.

[83] Selections 1856-8: 45

[84] W Thacker and Co. advert; Selections 1856-8: 45

[85] Selections 1856-8: 45

[86] Dalrymple 2007: 69

[87] Atkinson 1858: pls 9 & 12

[88] Selections 1854-6: 82

[89] Selections 1854-6: 82

[90] Atkinson 1858: pl.2

[91] Forrest 1893: 280

[92] See East India Register for 1857, entry dated April 1856.

[93] Robert James Atkinson appears in the so-called 'Mutiny circular' papers at L/MIL/10/119 pt.1: 127, British Library. James Augusts Atkinson can be found in *Who Was Who* 1953, Vol. 1: 28. and further details exist in Burke 1856: 229.

[94] L/MIL/10/64/436, Bengal Service Army Lists, British Library. James Pattle Beadle was on leave to Europe but Archibald Impey was in the thick of it. He *'accompanied the Field Force detached under Major Eyre to repel the* [unreadable] *of the mutineers from Oude'* and was further *'placed for special duty under the order of Capt. ?Yule?, Garrison Eng. of Allahabad S.O. 17 July '57. Transferred from the Darjeeling Road to the Allahabad Division P.W., G.O. 10 October 1857. Appointed to the temporary charge of the Engineer Park* [unreadable]*, from Allahabad with the advanced column from 4 Sep. G.O. 10th Nov. 1857* His record is reproduced here verbatim as it makes interesting reading when studied next to the 'Impey Letters' published in Taylor 1996: 3 in the entry for Agra. Impey merits further work and further details exist in his service records at the British Library.

[95] Blomfield 1992: xii

[96] Blomfield 1992: xii

[97] L/MIL/10/66/436, Bengal Service Army Lists, British Library. Atkinson 1859

[98] Atkinson 1859

[99] Atkinson 1859

[100] *The Morning Chronicle*, 23 April 1859, issue 28793

[101] *The Morning Chronicle*, 23 April 1859, issue 28793

[102] Forrest 1893: 279

[103] Hodson 1859: 215

[104] Anson 2004: 37

[105] East India Register 1857: 56

[106] *Illustrated London News*, 10 October 1857

[107] Hibbert 1983: 321

[108] Dalrymple 2007: 398

[109] If not Hodson then perhaps Major C Reid, officer commanding the Sirmoor Battalion of Gurkhas, but there are many possibilities and this story seems to have been well known at the time. See *Illustrated London News*, 10 October 1857: 373.

[110] W Thacker and Co. advert as in 92 above.

[111] L/MIL/10/119 pt. 1 p. 127, Mutiny Circular, British Library.

[112] See India Register 1858 p. 56 for his appointment and L/MIL/10/66/436, Bengal Service Army Lists, British Library, for his period of leave. This entry is slightly difficult to interpret as events seem to have overtaken him.

[113] *The Times*, Tuesday 2 November 1858: 9; Friday 10 December 1858: 7

[114] *The Morning Chronicle*, Wednesday, 15 December 1858, issue 28681

[115] *The Morning Chronicle*, Wednesday, 15 December 1858, issue 28681

[116] See India Register 1858 p. 56 for his appointment and L/MIL/10/66/436, Bengal Service Army Lists, British Library, for his period of leave. Bengal Service Army Lists, British Library.

[117] Letter by William Makepeace Thackeray as reproduced in the advert for W Thacker and Co. as in 110 above.

[118] Citation for 2nd Lt. Edward Talbot Thackeray *'For cool intrepidity and characteristic daring in extinguishing a fire in the Delhi Magazine enclosure, on the 16th of September, 1857, under a close and heavy musketry fire from the enemy, at the imminent risk of his life from the explosion of combustible stores in the shed in which the fire occurred'. London Gazette*, April 29 1862, p.2229.

[119] See letter from William Makepeace Thackeray to George Francklin Atkinson as referenced in 110 above.

[120] *Calcutta Review*, no. LXIV, December 1859: 306-16

References

Anson, O H S G 2004 *With H.M. Lancers during the Indian Mutiny; the letters of Brevet Major O H S G Anson*. Uckfield, Naval and Military Press

Atkinson, G F 1859 *Indian spices for English tables, or, A rare relish of fun from the Far East: Being, the adventures of "our special correspondent" in India, illustrated in a series of one hundred and twenty humorous sketches*. London, Day & Son

Atkinson, G F 1858 *Curry and Rice on Forty Plates: Or the Ingredients of Social Life at "Our Station" in India*. London, Thacker and Co.

Atkinson, G F (*ed.*) 1855 *The Delhi sketchbook* Delhi, Delhi Gazette Press, Delhi

Atkinson, G F 1848 *Pictures from the North in pen and pencil; sketched during a summer ramble*. London, John Olliver

Atkinson, J 1842 *The expedition into Afghanistan: notes and sketches descriptive of the country contained in a personal narrative during the campaign of 1839 & 1840 up to the surrender of Dost Mahomed Kahn* London, Wm. H. Allen & Co.

Boase, F 1965 *Modern English biography*. Vol. IV, A-C supp. to Vol. I. London, Frank Cass

Blomfield, D 1992 (*ed.*) *Lahore to Lucknow; The Indian Mutiny journal of Arthur Moffat Lang*. London, Leo Cooper

Bulletins and Other State Intelligence 1841 London, F Watts

Burke, E 1856 *The annual register or a review of the history and politics of 1855*. London, J Rivington

Burke, J (*ed.*) 1846 *The Patrician*. London, Churton

Crawford, D G 1914 *Roll of the Indian Medical Service 1615–1930* London, W Thacker and Co.

Dalrymple, W 2006 *The last mughal; the fall of a dynasty, Delhi 1857*. London, Bloomsbury

David, S 2002 *The Indian Mutiny*. London, Penguin

D'Oyly, C and **Atkinson, J** 1825 Tom Raw, the Griffin: a burlesque poem in twelve cantos by a civilian and an officer of the Bengal establishment. *The Naval and Military Magazine*, Vol. 1, 2nd ed.

Forrest, G W 1893 *The Indian Mutiny 1857–58; Selections from the letters, despatches and other state papers preserved in the military department of the government of India 1857–58*. Calcutta, Military Department Press

Hibbert, C 1983 *The Great Mutiny; India 1857*. London, Penguin

Hodson, G H 1859 (3rd ed.) *Twelve years of a soldier's life in India: Being extracts from the letters of the late Major W S R Hodson B.A., Trinity College, Cambridge; First Bengal European Fusiliers, Commandant*

of Hodson's Horse. Including a personal narrative of the siege of Delhi and Capture of the King and Princes. London, John W Parker and Sons

Matthew, H C G and **B Harrison** (eds) 2004 *Oxford Dictionary of National Biography.* Oxford, Oxford University Press

Parry, S H J 1897 *An old soldier's memories.* London, Hurst and Blackett

Poole, M C C 1912 *Ballads of Burma, anecdotal and analytical/by 'Oolay'.* Illustrated by T Martin Jones. London, W Thacker

Selections from the records of the Government of India; General Report on the administration of the Punjab Territories from 1854–55 to 1855–56 inclusive; no. XVIII. Lahore, J F Williams

Selections from the records of the Government of India (Foreign Department) published by authority; General report on the administration of the Punjab Territories From 1856–57 to 1857–58 inclusive; Together with a brief account of the administration of the Delhi Territory from the re-occupation of Delhi up to May 1858 Lahore, Kunniah Lall, Chronicle Press

Sneyd, E ND *Reminiscences of the dreadful mutiny in India in 1857 Vol. 1: Narrative referring to the years 1853–57* Photo Eur. 44. British Library

Stocqueler, J H 1851 *The British Officer; his position, duties, emoluments and priveleges; being a digest and compilation of the rules, regulations, warrants and memoranda relating to the duties, promotion, pay and allowances of the officers in Her Majesty's service and in that of the Hon. East India Company.* London, Smith, Elder & Co.

Taylor, P J O (ed.) 1996 *A companion to the 'Indian Mutiny' of 1857* Delhi, Oxford University Press

United Service Journal and Naval Military Magazine 1840 Part II.

Urban, S 1844 *The Gentleman's Magazine.* Vol. XXI New Series January to June inclusive. London, Pickering, Bowyer, Nichols and Son

Ward, A 1996 *Our bones are scattered; the Cawnpore Massacres and the Indian Mutiny of 1857.* New York, Henry Holt and Co.

Who Was Who 1953 Vol. 1. London, Adam and Charles Black

Acknowledgements

We thank the British Library for permission to reproduce images from *Pictures from the North* and *Indian spices for English tables.* Gillian Waters, Vanessa Kyle, Beth Heald, Annabel Gaskin, Chris Mercer and Lyndsey Slaven (especially) have all helped, materially or otherwise, with the production of this text.

CAMPAIGN IN INDIA
1857-58.

FROM DRAWINGS MADE DURING THE EVENTFUL PERIOD OF THE GREAT MUTINY.

GEORGE FRANKLIN ATKINSON,
CAPTAIN, BENGAL ENGINEERS.

ILLUSTRATING THE MILITARY OPERATIONS BEFORE

DELHI

AND ITS NEIGHBOURHOOD.

WITH DESCRIPTIVE LETTER-PRESS.

Capt. G.F. Atkinson del.   J. Walter lith.

Day & Son, Lith.ₜₒ the Queen.

Nº 1 SEPOYS AT RIFLE PRACTICE.

LONDON, PUBLISHED JANUARY 1ˢᵗ 1859, BY
DAY & SON, LITHOGRAPHERS TO THE QUEEN.
GATE STREET, LINCOLN'S INN FIELDS.

To Her Most Gracious Majesty the Queen.

MADAM,

WHEN a remorselessly treacherous and rebellious foe sought to uproot the British Power in India, and by acts of deliberately-planned ferocity and fiendish cruelty strove to destroy every European and Christian in the land, the devoted heroism of a small but resolute force, who fought to maintain the rights of their Sovereign and the honour of England, was so far crowned with success as to stay the arm of the destroyer, wrenching from his grasp the stronghold of rebellion, and winning for them not only victory in the crime-stained streets of Delhi, but the proud satisfaction of YOUR MAJESTY'S gracious approval and heart-felt sympathy.

Though opposed to all but overpowering numbers, in long-continued, close, and deadly conflict, amidst scorching heat and withering pestilence, by night and day, that band of heroes, when the fate of India vibrated in the balance, would not suffer a thought of any other result than, under the blessing of Almighty God, a victorious one, that should re-establish the sway of YOUR MAJESTY'S sceptre in the most splendid province of the Empire.

Undeterred by the protracted hardships of the siege, assault, and capture of Delhi, the glorious victors hastened to the rescue of their beleaguered countrymen and their families in Oude, gathering fresh laurels on the way, and taking share in the rescue of the suffering but heroic garrison of Lucknow.

The following Sketches, imperfect as they are, which, by permission graciously accorded, I respectfully dedicate to YOUR MAJESTY, will perhaps afford a faint idea of some of the scenes which that gallant force went through in honour of their country and for love of their Queen.

I am,

MADAM,

With the most profound respect,

YOUR MAJESTY'S most faithful and devoted
Subject and Servant,

GEORGE FRANCKLIN ATKINSON,

Captain, Bengal Engineers.

LIST OF PLATES.

THE CAMPAIGN IN INDIA: 1857-58.

1.—SEPOYS AT RIFLE PRACTICE.

THE causes which led to the Mutiny of the Bengal Army will, in all probability, remain for ever a matter of conjecture. So many conflicting opinions are entertained regarding this terrible revolt, that it is impossible to arrive at any conclusion that can satisfactorily account for a disaster which, awful and appalling in its nature, has already been productive of much good. Like a fearful tempest it fell upon the land, scattering ruin and destruction around; but in the havoc it created, the air—impregnated with pestilential vapours—was cleared, and the long-impending storm has, we may all fervently hope, produced a calm,—not that dangerous calm which forebodes the coming gale, but a settled and abiding quiet, which may endure for ages to come.

There are many who profess to have foreseen the approaching disaster, and who attribute it entirely to the fatal acts of the Government in pampering the native soldiery by yielding to them in their every wish, and succumbing to them whenever they evinced opposition; by withdrawing from commanding officers all power and authority over their men, until the Sepoys recognized in them nought but a cipher;—to this, above all, it is conceived that the lax state of discipline in the Bengal army arose. But to this it is objected, that the Sepoys of the Madras and Bombay armies were subjected to an identical state of things as regards the power and influence of commanding officers, and that they, as armies, did not mutiny. Others consider that the vast extension of our territory during the last few years tended more than anything else to create a feeling of dissatisfaction in the army. Men whose homes were in Oude, and who had hitherto been able to enjoy the opportunity of spending their leave with their families, from whom they were never separated by any extraordinary distance, now found themselves ordered away to be quartered for years in Scinde, or the Punjab, or in Burmah, without any corresponding advantages: but this feeling of dissatisfaction might have smouldered for ever; and though a spark of mutiny may have flashed here and there, such alone would never have ignited the whole army into a blaze of rebellion.

Then there are those who clearly recognize the cause of the Mutiny in the annexation of Oude, and maintain that the agents of the Royal family, knowing accurately the disaffected state of the native troops, found in them willing tools by which they could accomplish their own crafty ends; that they found the army conscious of its might, fully ripe for revolt, and they only bided their time until some fitting opportunity should occur. Nor had they long to wait. It is well known how tenacious is the Sepoy of his *caste*, and how suspicious he is of anything that is likely to affect his religion. The greater part—probably four-fifths—of the army being Hindoos, and more than half of these being Brahmins, known to be the most bigoted of their race, their influence was paramount; and, credulous to a degree as is the native mind, it was only for the agents of the Oude Royal family to obtain some plausible tale that it was the intention of the British Government to force them to adopt Christianity, and then the overthrow of British supremacy was a mere matter of time.

A pretext was readily afforded them by the introduction into the native army of the new Enfield rifles, the cartridges of which were made up with a mixture of cows' fat and hogs' lard, to taste which was sufficient to destroy the Sepoys' caste; and however varied may be the opinions regarding the original causes that tended to the great Mutiny, there is but one universally entertained, that the torch which created the conflagration was this matter of the greased cartridges. Whether the weapon was handled by the agents of the King of Oude, or by any other ambitious and designing native princes, may remain a conjecture; whether the state of the army was ripened to revolt by the disaffection arising from the extended frontier, or from want of power in the hands of the European officers, or from any other causes, there is no question about it, that the native army were impressed with the idea that it was the object of the Government to coerce them into the profession of Christianity, and that the new Commander-in-Chief had been sent from England expressly for the purpose of carrying it out. The sensation thus created was of no ordinary kind, and wise men clearly saw that some terrible disaster would befall if the use of the cartridges was persisted in.

This is not the place, however, for entering more fully into the events that occurred from the time when the 19th regiment broke into open mutiny, on the 25th of February, when it positively refused to receive the cartridges, until the memorable 10th of May, when the storm burst at Meerut with all its violence: suffice it to say, that from January to May the matter of the greased cartridges was unquestionably the pretext for the insurrection, and that through it the credulous minds of the Sepoys were thoroughly impressed with the idea (to such an extent that no arguments of their officers could in any way dissipate it) that they were to be Christianized; and rather than submit to this, they joined heart and hand in endeavouring to overthrow the British power, and massacre every Christian in the country.

The Government, early in 1857, had established at the principal stations Schools of Musketry, where detachments from every regiment in the service were sent to become instructed in the use of the new weapon. The Vignette represents a party of Sepoys who have joined at practice, and to whom has been communicated the nature of the cartridges.

THE
CAMPAIGN IN INDIA
1857-58.

FROM DRAWINGS MADE DURING THE EVENTFUL PERIOD OF THE GREAT MUTINY.

BY

GEORGE FRANKLIN ATKINSON,

CAPTAIN, BENGAL ENGINEERS.

ILLUSTRATING THE MILITARY OPERATIONS BEFORE

DELHI

AND ITS NEIGHBOURHOOD.

WITH DESCRIPTIVE LETTER-PRESS.

Nº 1. SEPOYS AT RIFLE PRACTICE

LONDON:PUBLISHED JANUARY 1st 1859 BY
DAY & SON, LITHOGRAPHERS TO THE QUEEN.
GATE STREET LINCOLNS INN FIELDS.

2.—THE FIRST BENGAL FUSILIERS MARCHING DOWN FROM DUGSHAI.

THIS Sketch represents the March of the 1st Bengal Fusiliers from the Hill station of Dugshai for the Plains, to join the force assembling at Umballa for the purpose of retaking the city of Delhi from the hands of the mutineers.

Dugshai is one of three military stations situated on the first range of the Himalayahs, and is about 7,000 feet above the level of the sea. The other two stations are Subathoo and Kussowlie, each situated at a distance of ten miles from each other. Kussowlie being nine miles from the foot of the hills, is reached by a steep and narrow road; further on, but at a lower level, not above 4,500 feet above the sea, is situated Subathoo, on the road to Simla, which is twenty miles further north. To connect Simla with the Plains by a road accessible for wheeled vehicles, a new line was traced, which, leaving Kussowlie and Subathoo, passed near the station of Dugshai, at a distance of twenty miles from the Plains.

Subathoo for many years had been the quarters of a local battalion of Hill-men called Goorkahs (a race of men who have highly distinguished themselves wherever they have been engaged), when Lord Ellenborough, as Governor-General, observing the advantage of locating the British troops in the cool and invigorating climate of the Himalayahs, removed the Goorkah battalion to new quarters close to Simla, and caused barracks to be erected at Subathoo and Kussowlie.

Finding the benefit that followed this arrangement, a third station was a few years later selected at Dugshai, which is situated on a bare and lofty mountain, but which, though not so attractive, from want of foliage, is nevertheless the most salubrious of the three, and from its position might with very slight fortifications be made a Gibraltar of the Himalayahs.

It was at these three stations that the British infantry, that fought so gallantly at Delhi, were quartered when the tidings came of the revolt at Meerut of the 10th May. On the 12th an aide-de-camp galloped through Kussowlie conveying the intelligence to General Anson, then at Simla: that same afternoon Her Majesty's 75th marched off from Kussowlie for Umballa, and on the following day the 1st Fusiliers received instructions to follow with the utmost expedition. In two hours the regiment was under arms, and in light marching order, without jackets, started joyfully on their mission, amidst cheers which will never be forgotten by those who heard them.

This gallant regiment, on whose colours are emblazoned the names of battles fought and won, from Plassey down to the taking of Burmah, marched gladly forth to reap that harvest of laurels which they successively gained both at Delhi and Lucknow. How they bore the brunt of many a hard-fought field, the following pages will tend to show; and the list of casualties, which by the official returns show that 319 fell or were wounded out of 427, tells its own tale.

The regiment marched that night thirty miles; and a trying time was it for men who, from a cool English climate, were suddenly brought down to encounter the fiery heat of a May day in the burning plains of India, with no protection for them but the shade of a few small trees, under which they bivouacked. The following day found them in Umballa at the end of their sixty miles march.

The 2nd Fusiliers, who were quartered at Subathoo, followed on the succeeding day; and these were the three weak British regiments of foot who, with the assistance of 400 of Her Majesty's 60th Rifles, upheld the honour of Old England for so many weeks before Delhi, and who, amidst pestilence and the terrors of a withering climate, fought so desperately and so successfully against such fearful odds.

3.—OFFICERS JOINING THE FORCE.

In consequence of the heavy loss which was experienced in officers during the continuous actions before Delhi, it was found necessary to apply to the local Government of the Punjab to spare as many officers as they could from regiments not engaged before Delhi; and gladly was the opportunity taken advantage of by all who were permitted to exchange the monotony of a quiet station life for the activity of real useful service, and especially when each man felt that his quota of assistance aided the force whose very existence was threatened by its constant casualties, and which so urgently needed an augmentation of power. The Sepoys well knew the value of officers, and, exposed as they were in the foremost and thickest of the danger, it is not surprising that the loss among them was excessive: one regiment—the Punjab Guides—was thrice cleared of all its officers; and many other corps suffered almost similarly. The Sketch represents the common mail-cart, which was gladly made use of, as being the most expeditious mode of transit; and on this rude and shaky contrivance for hundreds of miles were British officers to be seen incessantly passing on to the scene of action, by day and night hurrying on, only afraid they should be too late to take part in the grand assault which had been expected to come off at any time by a *coup de main*, and which it would have been galling to miss.

When the roads are good,—and this, the Grand Trunk Road, which extends from Calcutta to Peshawur, is, with few exceptions, a first-rate metalled road for a distance of some 1,000 miles,—the carts are drawn by one horse or rather pony, and travel at the average rate of ten miles an hour, including stoppages. Where the roads have not been metalled, —which is done by macadamizing them with a substance called kunkur, obtained in certain localities at a few feet below the surface of the ground, and which, when moistened and then carefully rammed, forms a beautifully hard and level surface,—the carts have a supplementary pony attached. A light awning, supported by two rods and strapped down over transverse strips of bamboo, affords some trifling mitigation from the scorching rays of the sun. But the carts are of the rudest construction, and the springs cannot boast of much elasticity; so that a journey on a mail-cart is reckoned a feat rather worthy of commemoration. The ponies are invariably either vicious or badly broken in, and the delays of starting have to be compensated for by increased velocity in speed: the rate (for the change occurs at every five miles) is generally, when in progress, some twenty miles an hour at the very least.

4.—A SCENE IN CAMP.

The British soldier who has been accustomed to the small bell-tents of a European encampment is somewhat struck when he first sees the expanse of canvas and the extent of ground occupied in the encampment of a British regiment in India. It is not, however, so much in the tents of the private soldiers (which are not one inch too large for the accommodation of the twelve men for whom they are intended), but it is in the tents of the officers. Commanding officers frequently have a large double-poled tent, measuring thirty feet by sixteen feet; besides one or two other smaller ones, usually single-poled, from fourteen to sixteen feet square; besides an awning and tents for the servants and horses. No fixed rule is adhered to,—every man provides himself as he pleases; and the only necessity that exists, is that the tents must all be pitched with a degree of uniformity, when the nature of the ground will allow of it. The prevailing kind of tent—and Bengal is so celebrated for its tents that it supplies the other two presidencies—is a single-poled tent, about fourteen feet square, with an outer fly or covering, and an outer wall, or *kunaut*, which gives a verandah of from two to three feet in width.

Subalterns, however, are generally content with a smaller kind, commonly called a hill tent, such as is represented in the Drawing: it is usually ten feet square, with a double roof but only single walls, and therefore with no verandah; but a strip of canvas extends over the sides a few feet, as a protection from the sun for servants: such a tent can be carried by a single camel. The Sketch also shows the manner in which horses are picketed. A rope is fastened to each hind fetlock, and is attached to a peg driven in the ground some few feet to the rear (this prevents the horse from either advancing or going sideways beyond a certain point), whilst to his halter are attached two head-ropes fastened to pegs right and left of him.

The figures in the foreground are enjoying the *otium cum dignitate* in the open air at a time when the sun's rays will admit of such a luxury.

Capt. G. F. Atkinson, del.   London, Day & Son, Lithographers to the Queen & to the late the King of Saxony   Plate 29.

5.—TROOPS HASTENING TO UMBALLA.

THE Grand Trunk Road, as has been already stated, is the main artery of communication between Calcutta on the east and Peshawur at the north-western extremity of the Indian empire. On this main line, or contiguous to it, are the principal Stations of the Bengal Presidency; and the amount of traffic is proportionately large. The extent of railway completed up to this time has been of little or no assistance towards facilitating the transport of merchandise, which, up to Allahabad, a distance of 400 miles by land, can likewise be conveyed on the Ganges, either in country boats, or on steamers, or on flats towed by steam-tugs. This distance is 800 miles by water, owing to the circuitous course of the river; and although only 400 miles by road, the time occupied in conveying goods averaged from twenty-five to thirty days. Above Allahabad, the only mode of transport was by native carts, which averaged ten miles a day; so that goods that had to be conveyed—say to Delhi, 800 miles from Calcutta—took upwards of ten weeks.

To remedy this dilatory state of things, Dr. Paton, who was postmaster at Allyghur, and to whom also may be attributed the introduction of the mail-cart system, and the accelerated rate of speed, proposed to establish carts between Allahabad and Delhi, to be drawn by bullocks, of which there were to be relays at every ten miles. The scheme was at once adopted, and through its instrumentality goods that occupied ten weeks from Calcutta to Delhi are now conveyed at a uniform average rate of two miles an hour, which reduced the time of transit to seventeen days.

Not only merchandise, but Government stores, and even troops, were forwarded by this " Bullock-train;" and many officers with their families have, after fitting up these carts, made use of them as travelling-carriages, to obviate the more dilatory and expensive process of marching, which involves the purchase of tents and the entertainment of much extra establishment.

The Bullock-train had been extended to Lahore, with a branch running from Umballa to Simla, when the outbreak took place; and, as may be supposed, advantage was at once taken of the opportunity thus afforded of making it useful for the transport of troops to the Camp. The rebels destroyed the carts, and took possession of the cattle, in the neighbourhood of Delhi; but by the assistance of the troops in the service of the Jheend and Puttialah Rajahs, the road was kept free from rebels, and the Bullock-train reorganized; and throughout the operations before Delhi it proved to be of the utmost importance for the conveyance of troops, who were thus landed at Delhi comparatively fresh. The Sketch represents the style of cart employed, the fore wheels being of the same diameter as the hind ones, and the roof covered with tarred canvas, the sides also being protected by tarpaulins.

Elephants, bazar ponies, and every kind of vehicle likewise, were immediately put into requisition to expedite the movement of troops.

6.—MUTINEERS SURPRISED BY HER MAJESTY'S 9TH LANCERS.

WITH the exception of the European Horse Artillery, of which there were two troops, the 9th Lancers was the only European regiment quartered at Umballa at the outbreak of the Mutiny.

A finer and a better-disciplined regiment was perhaps never seen: it numbered about 700 sabres, and the men, as they afterwards proved themselves to be, were as gallant and distinguished in the field as they were orderly in the cantonment.

This drawing represents a scene which occurred on the march of the force from Umballa to Delhi, and which was subsequently of frequent occurrence.

Large parties of rebel Sepoys were making away with *loot* or plunder, and had strings of *hackeries,* or native carts, piled up with treasure, which had been ransacked from the bungalows at Delhi and the adjoining stations. Mess plate, crockery, ladies' dresses, &c. &c., were heaped rudely together, to be sorted and divided at some more fitting opportunity.

The Sepoys one and all were no doubt in great glee at being the happy possessors of so much valuable spoil,—when lo! a small cloud of dust is seen rising in the far-off distance,—and rapidly it approaches,—nearer and nearer it comes, when the tramp of hoofs is heard, and the white dresses of horsemen are seen shining in the sun. There is no time for thought,—no time to yoke the bullocks that still are feeding, and to remove the carts from off the high road, and so escape observation. The Sepoys are numerous,—the approaching force is small; but they have white faces, and resistance would be of no avail; but there is no time for discussion,—the advanced guard of the cavalry catch sight of the rebels, and with drawn swords and lances at rest, they apply the spur, and in a twinkling are upon them.

That evening's sun sees that belt of trees with a rebel swinging from every bough. A drum-head court-martial has convicted them one and all. A small native cart is brought under a tree,—the rope is fastened to the rebel's neck and the overhanging branch,—the cart is suddenly driven on, and the miscreant left to swing.

D

7.—STORMING THE BATTERIES AT BADLE SERAI.

It had been a matter of fear in the camp of the small British force which was on its way from Umballa to recapture Delhi, that the rebels would not fight, and that no opportunity would be afforded of bringing upon them that summary vengeance which they so well merited for their diabolical acts at Meerut and Delhi. Intelligence, however, reached the camp that the enemy had intrenched themselves a few miles out of the city, and were preparing to dispute the onward march of our troops. This intelligence proved to be correct, and arrangements were accordingly made for attacking the rebel batteries. At one A.M. of the 8th June, the British troops marched from their encamping, in order to reach the enemy at daybreak. The force was divided into three small brigades; the first under Brigadier Showers, consisting of H.M.'s 75th regiment and the 1st Fusiliers, who were to deploy to the right of the road; the second brigade, composed of the 2nd Fusiliers, 60th Rifles, and Sirmoor Battalion, which was to take the left; and a brigade, consisting of H.M.'s 9th Lancers and some horse artillery, were to make a *détour*, cross the canal by a bridge lower down, and cut off the retreat of the enemy; while the few heavy guns were to remain in the centre, on the road, and the light batteries to operate on either side.

The troops advanced, and ere the day had dawned, a heavy gun boomed, and a round shot flew down the road, carrying destruction in the British ranks, and giving notice of the proximity of the enemy's position. At once the brigade deployed into line, while the heavy guns replied to the enemy's fire; but, from superiority of metal and number of guns they had considerable advantage; having, moreover, the range perfect, and one of the first shots falling among the staff, killing Colonel Chester, the Adjutant-General, and Captain Russell, orderly officer, our artillery was evidently unable to silence the batteries, and fearful was the havoc among the British gunners; so recourse was had to the cold steel, and the 1st brigade were called up to advance. In the mean time, the General, finding that a heavy fire was directed on the advancing line from the gardens and inclosures to the right, detached the 1st Fusiliers to attack the mutineers, who were there in crowds, and so turn their left flank. Thus H.M.'s 75th foot alone was left to assault the batteries; and right steadily they advanced, although scarcely a man of it had ever before been under fire, which now was exceedingly heavy, the round shot flying thick into their line, followed by volleys of grape. Thus the regiment steadily advanced, Brigadier Showers, conspicuous on a white charger, riding coolly in advance, as if he was on parade. On he rode, till judging it to be the moment for a more rapid advance, he waved his sword and gave the welcome order, "75th, Charge!" and then with a cheer the regiment sprang forward at the double, amidst a storm of musketry and grape, and the main battery was taken.

The General, in his despatch, reported that the regiment was gallantly led by its commanding officer,—as, indeed, it was; but before him rode the gallant Brigadier, whose name was accidentally omitted, and whose distinguished coolness in action, and fearless bearing at all times, made him beloved by the men of his brigade, who, after storming the battery and gaining the heights immediately before Delhi, exhausted as they were, rose and gave him three hearty cheers.

8.—THE OUTLYING PICKET.

THE Sketch represents a portion of one of the outlying pickets, of which a number were necessarily established in the most advantageous points round the camp. For some weeks little or no protection whatever was afforded to the men, and it was to their own good rifles they could trust to having a clear ground in front of them; but gradually stones were collected, and with a few sand-bags or gabions a rude shelter was obtained. From behind these small light parapets many a rebel was laid prostrate. Many a time, flushed with intoxicating liquors, would large masses threaten to sweep away the picket; but the steady fire from the British soldier kept them at bay, though at times the assistance of a field-piece was required to drive them back, when the numbers were overwhelming, as they not unfrequently were.

In these pickets the men, harassed by incessant fightings and constant alarms, requiring them to turn out at all hours, were enabled to snatch a brief repose till those on the look-out warned them of an impending attack.

Exposed throughout the heat of the day, and during the wet season, to the heavy drenching rain, it is not to be wondered at that disease did as much execution as the fire of the enemy; but it was unavoidable, and every man knew it, and bore his share, not without a murmur only, but right gladly and cheerfully, watching with a wistful eye that long red wall, against which he was dying to be led, that he might come hand to hand with that fiendish race who, in cold blood, had butchered defenceless women and hacked to pieces the poor unoffending children.

9.—REPULSE OF A SORTIE.

DURING the earlier period of the siege operations before Delhi, the assaults of the mutineers on the advanced posts and batteries of the British line were incessant. It is true that the Sepoys very much preferred fighting behind walls and bringing down our exposed troops when they themselves were comparatively secure behind good cover, and it was very difficult to tempt them into the open; but although this was their prevailing system, there were many exceptions to it.

When the rebels, excited with intoxicating drugs, and compelled by their comrades in the city to go forth and attack the English camp, in order to show that they were true to the rebel cause,—and which ordeal every new comer had to go through before being admitted within the city gates,—on such occasions they were frequently induced to make real assaults. At first the British commanders led their men out of the trenches to attack the mutineers as they advanced; but as, in addition to being exposed to overwhelming numbers, and suffering heavily on each occasion from the guns on the city walls, the plan was changed and the men kept strictly on the defensive, this to the native mind implied fear; and the result was what was fully expected, that the rebels would show more pluck and advance right against the batteries, which they frequently did when they had an idea that the men occupying the post were but few in number or exhausted from fatigue. On these occasions, being well primed with *bang*, they would advance against our batteries; but not a shot would be fired, not a British soldier expose himself, till they began to swarm up the parapet, when, springing up with a volley and mounting the parapets, our gallant men would hurl themselves on to the mass of rebels and mete out summary slaughter, while those who fled were dosed with volleys of grape. The Sketch represents such an occurrence.

ON PICKET.

Capt. G. F. Atkinson, del.   London Day & Son Lithographer, to the Queen, Gate Street Lincoln's Inn Fields   E. Walker, lith.

THE SHELTER TRENCH.

10.—REINFORCEMENTS PROCEEDING TO DELHI.

THE very small force before Delhi, incessantly under fire, was decreasing in numbers so rapidly, while, on the other hand, the force of the enemy was daily and hourly acquiring fresh strength, that it became indispensable that no effort should be spared to push forward, with the utmost despatch, every single available soldier. A day—yes, even an hour—was of the greatest importance; for though each man was ready to yield his life rather than give in an inch, human nature could not long support a continuance of such fearful wear and tear. Exposure to the sun, and with no rest, day or night, except the few snatches of sleep that could be obtained when on duty at the pickets,—continually under a heavy fire, and constantly exposed to hand-to-hand conflicts with the enemy, no flesh could endure such a trial for any length of time; and the enemy knew this well, and, owing to their numbers, they were enabled to play their own game, and by incessant alarms and threatenings of assaults, the poor wearied British soldier was perpetually under arms. The alarm-bugle was for ever sounding, and it was becoming clear to every one that by reinforcements alone could there be any hope of taking Delhi; for it was as much as the English force could now do to hold their own. It was Sebastopol on a smaller scale, with a battle of Inkermann every other day. Every exertion was therefore made to push down troops; and among other devices resorted to was the one of carrying the soldiers in panniers slung on camels' backs. In these panniers, or *kujawahs*, the cooking utensils belonging to the companies were usually carried; but in each of these there was now stowed a soldier; and by this arrangement he was enabled to proceed some forty miles a day, instead of ten to fifteen, without any further fatigue than resulted from the awkward gait, and consequent uneven motion, of the camel.

The sick were still conveyed in *doolies*, of which one is represented in the foreground. It consists of a simple framework, with a string bottom, on which is laid a thin mattress, while the top and sides are closed in with a red covering of coarse cloth, the whole slung to a stout bamboo, and borne by four natives, of whom there were relays all along the road.

11.—HORSE ARTILLERY IN ACTION.

THE Horse Artillery of the Indian Army is on a very different system to that adopted in European armies. In the latter, the guns are drawn by four or six horses, driven by a gunner for every pair; while the remainder of the troop are mounted separately: by which means they are enabled to act as cavalry in defence of their guns. In the Indian Horse Artillery, a gunner is mounted upon every horse. Each system has its advocates; but unquestionably, so far as efficiency is concerned, nothing can apparently be more perfect than that of the Indian Horse Artillery in the field. In rapidity of movement, rapidity and accuracy in firing, and a wonderful facility of traversing the most broken ground, they are especially conspicuous. During the recent operations, the Commander-in-Chief spoke in the highest terms of admiration of this branch of the service, and repeated what had been so frequently acknowledged before, that the Indian Artillery was second to none, and even, in some respects, surpassed the distinguished artillery of the British army. Not that the officers or men of the Royal Artillery were one whit inferior, or their system imperfect; but they had been brought up in a different school, and from want of opportunities on actual field service, had not had recently any occasion to take their guns at full gallop over ditches and mud walls, and over the most rugged ground, at a pace that renders it difficult for light cavalry even to keep up with; while the Indian Horse Artillery, from constant opportunities in the field, have acquired the practice of getting across country in a style that astonishes every one who may never before have witnessed it.

The troops that belonged to the Delhi force particularly distinguished themselves, and frequently advanced so close to the walls as to draw the fire of the heavy guns upon them, and to which they replied with their light guns with startling effect. The full dress consists of blue, with gold lace, and a Roman helmet with a strip of leopard-skin round it, and having a crimson horse-hair plume. This was exchanged on service for a light pith helmet, covered with white, and with folds of cloth wound round it, and white jackets and pantaloons, which were gradually exchanged for the all-prevailing mud-colour. Each troop consists of four guns, either 6 or 9-pounders, and two 12-pounder howitzers. Before the outbreak, the Bengal Horse Artillery consisted of nine troops with European, and three troops with native gunners.

12.—INCIDENT IN THE SUBZEE MUNDEE.

As already mentioned, the men of the Sirmoor battalion are chiefly Goorkahs, a race of Hill-men, very small in stature, and with a cast of countenance bordering on that of the Chinese; high cheek-bones, small eyes, thick lips, and a complexion of a burnt sienna tinge.

These men are of the race that forms the chief force of the army of Nepal, and are descendants of those very men who fought so desperately against us in the Nepalese war: they are a hardy, valiant race of little warriors, cool in action, and with fiery courage in close encounter. During the Sutlej campaign they were a terror to the Sikhs, as, throwing aside their rifles, they drew their short sharp knives, and closed in upon the enemy. The Goorkahs during the whole siege of Delhi occupied the most advanced and the most exposed position on the heights, being quartered at Hindoo Rao's house, which was the key of the British position, and against which the enemy made daily assaults. The losses in the battalion, viz., 319 killed and wounded, out of 450, show how hard must have been their share in the dangers of the siege. More than once it was proposed to relieve them; but the men, like their gallant commanding officer, Major Reid, begged to be allowed to remain in their dangerous position, which they looked upon as the place of honour.

The Goorkahs have always had a predilection for the British troops, whom they highly respect, but have a signal contempt for the Sepoys, whom they despise, looking upon them as much their inferiors, and reckoning that one Goorkah is at any time a match for three of them.

The men are armed and dressed like the 60th Rifles, whom they had never seen until they met on this occasion, and with whom they at once fraternized in the most friendly manner; and an honourable rivalry was at once established between them. Posted on the same ridge, ever exposed to the fire of the enemy, men of both corps were constantly to be seen skirmishing and bringing down, at a distance of 1,800 yards, any rebel who dared to expose himself.

The Goorkahs are wonderful shots with their rifles, as indeed are the men of the 60th Rifles, who behaved throughout the operation with the most consummate and conspicuous bravery. The casualties in the latter regiment were 389 killed and wounded, of a force which numbered but 440, until a few days before the storm, when it was reinforced by 200 more.

Besides the rifle, the Goorkah is provided with a knife called a *koorkerie*,—a fearful weapon in his hand, as sharp as a razor; and wonderfully expert is the owner in handling it.

The Sketch represents an incident that occurred in the suburbs of Delhi called the Subzee Mundee, which is a village situated on the right of the British position, and which was filled with rebels on the first approach of the force, and from which it was most difficult to drive them out, owing to the innumerable inclosure-walls, gardens, and other cover, which prevented the proper advance of our troops. The village was, however, after much fighting, taken possession of, and a strong picket established there; but up to the very last it was the scene of constant fighting. On one occasion a party of the 2nd Bengal Fusiliers, who were chiefly engaged in that direction, had, with a few Goorkahs, swept down the street and taken possession of the village, when some of the men, with a single Goorkah, sat down to rest, when, from an adjoining window, a Sepoy, who had been concealed in a house, thought to take advantage of the silence to see what was going on. He looked out and stared up the street, when, quick as thought, he was observed by the little Goorkah, who at once sprung up, clutched him firmly by the top-knot on his head, whisked out his koorkerie, and, like a flash of lightning, sliced off his head, and then quietly sat down, as if nothing had happened, to the intense amusement of his British comrades.

13.—INTERIOR OF A TENT.

The exterior view of a hill tent has already been represented. This drawing shows an interior of one which might be thought, in the Delhi camp, to be rather of a superior kind; for it must be remembered that the movements of the troops were so rapid, and anything like a march at that season of the year had so little entered into the imagination of any one, that no preparations whatever could be made, and those who, at other times, indulged in double or single-poled tents, were now unable, from want of carriage, to take them on; and so the smallest tents, such as are commonly used for dressing in or given up to servants, were gladly made use of, and the bazars were ransacked of everything that bore even a resemblance to a canvas abode. Thus the officers of the 1st Fusiliers were, from the haste of their departure, unable to take their tents, and they were all huddled together in one large double-poled one, whilst many were only too glad to get hold of a common soldier's tent.

The Sketch then represents one that rejoices in a *setringee*, or floor-cloth, and in *chicks*, or reed curtains, at the doors, to keep out the flies, which, at Delhi, are a perfect plague. The heat is terrific; the tent is pitched on a sandy piece of ground, and the sun beats right through the thick double roof; the thermometer stands at 118° of heat. The only resource is to wrap the head in a towel and keep it saturated; and incessantly has the attendant slave to be summoned to provide a fresh supply of water, as the heat soon makes the towel as dry as chalk. Then, as an additional refuge, the bed is hoisted up on to the camel-trunks, and beneath its thick mattress there is some slight modification of the direct rays of the sun; but still the heat is prodigious. In vain letters are attempted to be written—the ink has dried up—the pens have split; and then there goes the alarm—again it sounds—no time to be lost; the sword is seized from its sheath, which is left behind,—the revolver is laid hold of,—the turbaned helmet is clapped on, and away, right under the burning sun, rushes forth the gallant hero, regardless of heat, or aught that could impede him in his duty.

Nº 12. INCIDENT IN THE SUBZEE MUNDEE

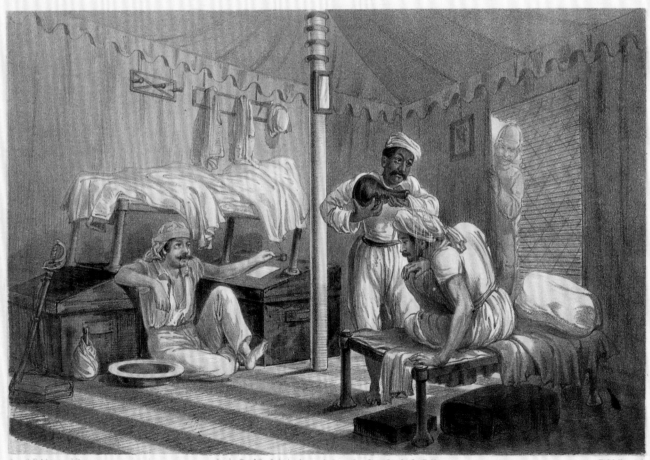

Capt. G. F. Atkinson delt.   London Day & Son Lithographers to the Queen, Gate Street Lincoln's Inn Fields   E. Walker lith.

Nº 13. INTERIOR OF A TENT

14.—HODSON'S HORSE AT RHOTUCK.

AMONG the many heroes who distinguished themselves during the operations before Delhi, none was more conspicuous than the gallant HODSON, whose glorious achievements had won for him a world-wide reputation. In India his name had long been known as commanding the corps of Guides on the North-west frontier, with which, in countless frays and forays with the wild Hill races, his feats of valour had rendered him and his gallant Guides the terror of the neighbouring disaffected tribes. Removed from his command, and compelled to join his regiment, the 1st Bengal Fusiliers, as a subaltern, he led, what was to him, a life of painful inactivity, until the mutiny broke out, when the Commander-in-Chief appointed him to raise and command a new regiment of horse, to number 2,000 sabres, and which was to bear his name. That name of Hodson was quite sufficient, in the Punjab, to bring to his standard hundreds of gallant Sikhs, who gladly sought to be under his orders. Troops were soon organized at Lahore and elsewhere, and hastened to join the force at Delhi, where Hodson now was acting on the Commander-in-Chief's staff, as also in the Quartermaster-General's department; not, however, before he had again distinguished himself by conveying despatches to the General at Meerut, across country some eighty miles, through the midst of the rebels. How Hodson was ever foremost in the thickest of every encounter would fill a volume; mention need only be made here of the affecting meeting that took place between him and his old companions in arms, the gallant Guides, who (a body of horse and foot) had marched from Peshawur to Delhi, a distance of 600 miles, in the unprecedentedly short space of twenty-two days, and joined in a desperate engagement on the very afternoon of their arrival.

With a party of the cavalry portion of the Guides and a squadron of his own Horse, Hodson, with 300 sabres and six officers, sallied forth from camp to intercept a body of rebels who had left Delhi to interrupt our communications with the Punjab. On the first march he surprised and destroyed a party of mutineer irregular cavalry, and then proceeded to Rhotuck, where he found the enemy in no great force, who were soon scattered; and he and his party took up their quarters for the night in the town. Thinking to make an easy capture of Hodson and his small force, a disaffected Rajah, Babur Khan, collected during the night a horde of rebels, both cavalry and infantry, the greater portion being mutineers from our own irregular cavalry and native regiments, and surrounded the place; but Hodson, who had previously sent off his little baggage, and with horses ready saddled, waited his opportunity to sally out. The enemy's cavalry dashed up boldly to the camp, when Hodson's squadrons speedily scattered them, and drove them back.

Then it was that, seeing the numbers of matchlock-men that were brought to bear on his party from gardens and enclosures, he determined to draw them out, and feigned a retreat. The *ruse* was most successful. He had scarcely retired a mile, when the enemy, in full force, with all the pride of anticipated victory, came after him, flourishing their swords in the air and yelling triumphantly, when Hodson, who had now got them into the open plain, gave the words, "Threes about at them!" when he and his men, with a cheer, dashed into the very thickest of them, cutting down fifty in half that number of seconds, and scattering the rest, who fled with dismay.

15.—HEAVY DAY IN THE BATTERIES.

WHEN the British force first took possession of the heights in the immediate vicinity of Delhi, batteries were at once erected for the few heavy guns that had been brought with the force from Umballa, and those taken from the enemy at the Hindun and at Badle-Serai. These batteries were erected at various points along the ridge, at a range varying from 1,500 to 2,000 yards from the walls. The one in the Sketch represents a portion of one near an old mosque, which was situated about the centre of the ridge, midway between the Flagstaff Battery and Hindoo Rao's. The efforts of the enemy were principally directed against the batteries nearer Hindoo Rao's, which were more accessible; but the position, even at the Mosque Battery, was far from enviable, as the practice of the enemy was wonderfully accurate, even at that long range, and two of our howitzers were soon dismounted by them. The gunners of the British force were so few, that the duty imposed on them rendered it quite impossible for our guns to cope successfully against those of the rebels, whose artillery was of far heavier calibre, and who had an inexhaustible supply of ammunition, and men in abundance to work the guns. With superiority of fire, coupled with unceasing attacks on the British camp and batteries, to harass and exhaust the few troops that defended them, was the object the rebels had in view; and this was, perhaps, never more closely on the eve of being successfully accomplished than on the eventful anniversary of Plassey, when the whole strength of the garrison was put forth to overwhelm the British troops, already well-nigh exhausted with incessant fighting and exposure. From daybreak till sunset was one continued conflict under a burning sun: skirmishing and hand-to-hand encounters took place along the whole right of the camp for hours consecutively. But the story can best be told in the words of a distinguished officer, who played a very conspicuous part on that, as, indeed, on every day, from the action of Badle-Serai until a desperate wound, six weeks later, compelled him for a time to cease from taking any share in the operations. He wrote:—" All our troops had now been engaged, and the greater part had fallen back exhausted. The General then directed me to the Mosque Battery, where applications were being constantly sent for reinforcements: I sent every available man. I was then directed to assume command at Hindoo Rao's: when I arrived there, I found every one exhausted and done up;—there were the 1st Fusiliers and some Rifles, all done up. I went on to the new advanced battery,—it was crowded with worn-out men; the artillerymen, likewise done up, had ceased firing; another party of Rifles, in a similar state, in another position; 120 men of the 2nd Fusiliers, who had marched twenty-three miles that morning, and had had no breakfast, were lying down exhausted; three weak companies of Goorkhas were out as skirmishers; but they, too, were exhausted, and the remainder were resting under a rock. The heat was terrific, and the thermometer must have been at least 140°, with a hot wind blowing, and a frightful glare. Well, the mutineers all this time, from behind walls and rocks, were keeping up a brisk fire all along our front, *i.e.* to the right of Hindoo Rao's house, as far as Subzee Mundee, and a battery of two guns from Kissengunj was firing upon us without having it returned. I ordered up, when at Hindoo Rao's, 100 of the 1st Fusiliers: after serving out grog to them, I threw them forward to the left front of the new battery. I got a reinforcement of 200 of Rothney's Sikhs, who also had marched twenty-three miles, and had as yet nothing to eat; and shortly afterwards a small party of 30 of the 2nd Fusiliers, and another under the Sergeant-Major. The latter was sent with the 1st Fusiliers: they beat back the mutineers at once, and took possession of a temple on the left front of the batteries, and which commanded it. On the right I threw forward Rothney's Sikhs, some Guides, and a few of the 2nd Fusiliers: they advanced, and again took possession of Subzee Mundee. Between this and the batteries our skirmishers now had command of the whole ground; we were now masters of the field,—the mutineers were completely beaten; and when they found I intended to hold my position, they fell back upon the town. Our loss was considerable,—160 killed and wounded; but that of the enemy was very severe. We suffered greatly from the sun: the 1st Fusiliers alone had five officers out of ten struck down by *coup de soleil.*"

Such is a specimen of the kind of work that the British had to undergo from the 8th of June to the 13th of September; and small as was the force for the first six weeks,—numbering about 7,000 men of all arms,—the casualties during that time were 22 officers and 296 men killed, and 72 officers and 990 men wounded.

16.—FUSILIERS BRINGING THE CAPTURED GUNS INTO CAMP.

THE enemy, having about the latter end of July obtained a vast accession of strength, had assumed a more than ordinary degree of boldness, and their efforts were constantly being directed to force the British advanced pickets on the left,—that is, the stable, mound, cow-house, and other pickets in the neighbourhood of the Metcalfe House. These faced the Cashmere Bastion; and not content with attacks of infantry, the rebels had caused considerable damage by bringing out field-pieces, which sent round-shot and grape thick among our men. To put a stop to this, Brigadier Showers was directed to make arrangements for getting possession of their guns; and accordingly, on the morning of the 12th August, he sallied forth with a small force, consisting of 350 men of the 1st Fusiliers and 250 of Coke's Rifles (which two corps bore the chief brunt of the engagement); 100 of the 2nd Fusiliers, of the 8th Foot, Goorkahs, and 4th Sikhs; 100 of H. M.'s 75th, who were on picket at the Metcalfe House, and, accompanied with six guns of horse artillery and a squadron of the 9th Lancers, stole quietly down into the neighbourhood of the enemy, who, in unconscious security, had not withdrawn their guns into the city, but had them all ready for an attack on the British lines that very morning. But the Brigadier was too early for them: ere the day had dawned, the mud-coloured—and therefore difficult to be distinguished—British troops quietly approached, till the rebel sentry calling out, "Hoo kum dar?" (Who comes there?) was replied to by a bayonet thrust through him: but the alarm was given, the rebels sprung to their arms, and a hand-to-hand conflict ensued. Suffice to say that the action lasted about an hour, that an advance was made, and gun after gun captured, the rebel artillerymen being bayoneted beside them.

The little expedition was well planned by Brigadier Showers, and was so secretly performed, that those in camp were first apprized of it by the cheering which greeted the victors as they brought into camp, at a gallop, the guns that had just been retaken by them. The scene was as novel as amusing; to behold the horses mounted by infantry, each man carrying his musket with the blood-besmeared bayonets, and urging on the horses at full speed, with a reckless amount of expedition; the limber and guns encrusted also with infantry, who were enjoying the ride home; young OWEN, a subaltern of the 1st Fusiliers, who had been wounded on the occasion, occupying a prominent position.

This little action was one of the most successful in the operations before Delhi, and reflected the highest credit on the Brigadier and all who fought under him. Unfortunately the Brigadier was very severely wounded by a bullet in his chest; but he refused to quit the field, although the General, hearing of it, had sent another officer to relieve him, if he wished. It was not until he had received a second wound, in the hand, and he saw the object of the day gained by the carrying of the guns, that, weak with loss of blood, he gave up the command.

The losses on that morning, considering the sharp nature of the action, were comparatively trifling, being 1 officer and 19 men killed, and 7 officers and 85 men wounded; but the effects of the action were plain, as the pickets were no longer molested by artillery; for the rebels felt that to bring them out of the city gates was simply to insure their being captured.

17.—SEARCH FOR THE WOUNDED.

THIS Sketch represents the field of action, when, after an engagement, a search is being made for the killed and wounded. On many occasions before Delhi, it was impossible to remove the wounded as they fell; often the engagement was carried on in such broken ground, that an advance in any regular formation was impossible, and every man was left to fight his own way along;—thus numbers fell, and were only missed when the column returned to camp. Then had search to be made, and fortunate was it if a wounded man was found alive; for, like vultures, the mutineers, from their overwhelming numbers, hovered round as our men retired, and ruthlessly butchered the wounded, and hacked their bodies in pieces. Thus one officer, who was known to have fallen from his horse by a shot through his thigh, but who could not be removed at the time, was sought for in vain that night: but when day broke, his body was found hacked to pieces.

The Sketch represents a party somewhat more fortunate, as the wounded men have not been attacked by the butchers. The principal figure is a horse-artilleryman, who has found, and is carrying to camp, his poor brother, from whom life has passed away. He is telling, with a throbbing heart, and big tears rolling down his cheeks, to a young ensign, who has questioned him how it happened, the story of his poor brother, and what affliction it will cause his old mother at home, but that he hopes to avenge his loss; and he is somewhat gratified at recollecting that the last round of grape he had the satisfaction of pouring into the retreating mass of rebels, brought down the author of his calamity.

18.—SAPPERS AT WORK IN THE BATTERIES.

THE Sappers and Miners of the Bengal Army consisted, before the outbreak, of ten companies of Sepoys, who were instructed by their European officers in all the details of that branch of the profession to which they were devoted. When the outbreak took place at Meerut, reinforcements were summoned from every direction; and among them the Sappers and Miners, who had their head-quarters at Roorkee, on the Ganges Canal, not far from Meerut, were ordered in forthwith. Their commanding officer, the gallant Captain Fraser, had implicit confidence in the fidelity of his men, and felt assured that, though the rest of the army might rebel, his corps would yet remain true to their allegiance. But, poor fellow, his confidence was ill-founded; for the corps mutinied, and Fraser was shot dead by his own men.

The greater portion, or about 400, who escaped from the sword of the carabinier, made off straight for Delhi, leaving about 150 of their number faithful to their salt. Such an addition of trained men to the rebel force was most invaluable; for by their aid were they enabled to construct and keep in repair those defensive works which so materially retarded our progress in the capture of the place. As for instance, on one occasion the concentrated fire of our heavy guns was brought to bear on a certain bastion: the fire, so well directed, dismounted the enemy's guns even at a range of 1,600 yards, and demolished the face of the works. An assault was in contemplation; but, when morning appeared, the bastion appeared stronger than ever; the injuries had been made good, and a larger number of guns, of still heavier calibre than before, soon sent their shot flying into the British batteries with unerring aim,—so well had the rebels been taught.

And yet it is strange, that, opposed to these were a small remnant of the faithful, who, to the last, worked in the British batteries exposed to the fire of their former comrades, with the greatest intrepidity. The numbers were so few, that a large party of canal-diggers were entertained in the Punjab, and engaged to work, under fire, in the trenches; and, in addition to these, a large body of common labourers were likewise engaged; and right gallantly did these novices to the art of war conduct themselves. Directed by a zealous, indefatigable body of young officers, and an able party of non-commissioned officers, who had been recalled from civil duties to devote themselves to their former occupation as Sappers and Miners, the works progressed, assisted by the British troops, who worked hard in the trenches and in the batteries. And severe work they say it was during the wet season, when the rain fell in sheets, saturating one to the skin, and exposed all the time to the accurate fire of the enemy, whose shells frequently pitched with admirable precision, and burst right in the midst of the working parties. But the works were pushed on, the killed and the wounded were removed, and the *fowrah*, or native spade, was plied more energetically than ever.

SAPPERS AT WORK IN THE TRENCHES

OFFICER SEARCHING FOR THE WOUNDED

19.—ADVANCE OF THE SIEGE TRAIN.

THIS Sketch represents the advance of the siege-train that was despatched to Delhi for the purpose of demolishing the fortifications, which, it was found, could not possibly be effected by means of the few heavy guns that originally accompanied the force on its first breaking ground before Delhi.

Anticipating but a trifling resistance, if any, on the part of the rebels, a very few guns were brought from Umballa: these, on the first outbreak of the mutiny, were in the magazine at the Fort of Phillour, under the charge of a Sepoy regiment; and it was feared that there would be difficulty in obtaining possession of them; but in consequence of a rapid night march of a wing of H.M.'s 8th Foot from the neighbouring station at Loodianah, the regiment was surprised, and the arsenal secured. An artillery officer was immediately despatched from Simla by the Commander-in-Chief to bring a third-class siege-train to Umballa, which was accordingly done, by dint of the greatest exertion, and was effected not one moment before it was necessary; as, immediately after the last gun had crossed the bridge of boats that spanned the then narrow stream of one of the Five Rivers, the water rose, in consequence of the melting of the snows in the Himalayahs, and carried away the bridge. These guns were drawn by bullocks, from eighteen to twenty-four being yoked to each piece.

When it was found that this small train was ineffective to demolish the enemy's works, and that the pieces suffered so much from the accurate practice of the rebel artillery, who dismounted several, even at a range of 1,700 yards, and that the guns were, moreover, injured by the incessant firing, a new siege-train was ordered to be sent from the arsenal of Ferozepore. This magazine being at a distance of nearly 200 miles from Delhi, created considerable delay in the taking of the city; for nothing could be done but for our troops to maintain themselves in their position until its arrival, which was not until the 7th of September; by which time the batteries had been duly prepared for their reception.

The guns of this train were drawn by elephants, as shown in the Drawing,—a single elephant attached to each; but at times, when the road was deep in sand, the assistance of a second elephant had to be brought into requisition; and, with a pad to protect his forehead, he would push the wheels, lowering himself on his knees, and showing wonderful sagacity in adopting the best mode of extricating the ponderous mass from its difficulties. The train consisted of nearly fifty pieces of heavy ordnance; and these, together with the innumerable carts of ammunition, extended over about seven miles of road, and were protected by British infantry, new Sikh levies, and some irregular cavalry.

20.—TROOPS OF THE NATIVE ALLIES.

AMIDST the force that was gradually increasing in numerical strength for the grand assault of the city of Delhi, was a motley array of troops belonging to different Rajahs who had faithfully adhered to the British cause; of whom the most conspicuous throughout the mutiny was the Rajah of Puttialah, whose territory lay in the neighbourhood of Umballa. It was one of the " Protected Sikh States" before the annexation of the Punjab; and in consequence of the adherence of the Rajah to the British, the state was not confiscated, but additional territory was granted to him as a reward for assistance rendered. When this mutiny broke out, the Rajah at once placed his troops at the disposal of the British Government; and it is not, perhaps, too much to say, that the safety of Northern India entirely rested on his faithfulness: for it was in his power to have cut off all communication between the Punjab and the Commander-in-Chief's force, which, but for his assistance, could never have reached Delhi; in fact, the small European force would have had its hands fully occupied in holding its own. The Jheend Rajah and others rendered most salutary assistance; but the most distinguished character in title was the Maharajah of Cashmere, who at once offered to place a force at our disposal. This offer was at first declined by the rulers of the Punjab, but was subsequently accepted, when it was discovered how essential it was that reinforcements should be supplied, to enable our small force to crush the enemy in his stronghold.

The army of the Cashmere Rajah was composed of different races of men; principally, however, was it recruited from the hills: it was supposed to be drilled according to European fashion; but for want of proper knowledge on the subject, the result was anything but advantageous. The moral effect, however, of having the Maharajah on our side, and the mere fact of his having sent a large force to assist in the subjugation of Delhi, was of immense importance, and operated most beneficially towards the object in view; and lucky for us was it that the moral power was of such advantage, as the positive good that the troops afforded was very questionable. The Sketch represents the troops on the march,—a very irregular body, as may be seen,—scarcely two habited alike, and with arms of every fashion and of every age. The guns were drawn by mules, the cavalry mounted on wretched ponies; and what with bullock-carts, camels, elephants, sheep, goats, tatoos, women, children, the looker-on would scarcely recognize an army intent upon any really hard work. Efficiency in the field could scarcely be expected; so that it was in no way surprising that, when led against the enemy's batteries, the men flinched and fell back, leaving the few British troops who accompanied them to bear the whole brunt of that desperate hand-to-hand conflict that took place at the Kissengunge on the morning of the assault, and which, owing to the flight of the native allies, rendered the attack in that quarter unsuccessful.

21.—THE STORMING OF DELHI.

On the eventful 14th of September, the grand assault of Delhi took place, which, though crowned with success, was not effected without a sanguinary struggle, involving casualties to the enormous extent of one-third of the force engaged. Although the British had encamped before the place ninety-seven days previously,—although batteries had been erected, and heavy guns had opened their fire upon the devoted city,—yet this was very soon found to be totally inadequate even to keep down the fire of the enemy, much less to demolish the defences: for ninety days, therefore, it may be fairly considered that the British force merely held its own ground until sufficient reinforcements, coupled with a more efficient siege-train, could be obtained. This was not effected until the ninetieth day, that is, on the 7th of September, when the operations of the siege fairly commenced; ground was broken that same evening, and on the morning of the 14th the assault was delivered: thus the reduction of the fortified portion of the city was consummated within a period of eight days.

The defences consisted of a massive wall, about 12 feet thick and 16 feet high, supporting a crenelated parapet, with occasional bastions of modern form, which were constructed by our Government some thirty years ago to improve and strengthen the original Mogul fortifications: these bastions carry each from six to fourteen guns. The whole *enceinte* on the land side is protected by a dry ditch, 24 feet wide and 20 feet in depth. The escarp is revêted with a masonry wall eight feet high, above which is a wide berm, from which rises the massive wall already alluded to.

The breaching batteries having been established, and fifty-four pieces of heavy ordnance having opened their destructive fire upon the points selected for assault, the enemy's guns were speedily silenced, and practicable breaches effected. Columns of attack assembled at daybreak, and were launched against the insurgents' defences, which, by means of escalade, blowing open of the Cashmere gate, and the direct assault of the open breaches, were speedily carried at the point of the bayonet.

But although the main fortifications were thus rapidly taken possession of, the hardest fighting and the most desperate struggles, calling forth the utmost courage and resolution of the gallant besiegers, had now to be encountered. Street-fighting is ever a dangerous and a slaughterous style of warfare, and in this instance was particularly so, as the extent of city that had to be traversed was unusually large; and, thoroughly defended, as was each nook and corner, from which musketry poured forth destruction into the ranks of the assailants, it is not surprising that it became the work of many days even for the resolute and daring men who thirsted to annihilate the defenders, who looked not for quarter, to accomplish.

Among the many desperate conflicts, perhaps none was more trying than that which is illustrated in the accompanying Drawing. The 1st brigade, consisting of a portion of the 75th Foot, the 1st Fusiliers, and the 2nd Punjab Rifles, personally led by the gallant Nicolson, had carried the principal bastion by assault, and re-forming behind the Cashmere gate, in the open space in front of the church, were directed to turn to the right, make a circuit of the walls, clearing the rampart as they advanced, with a view to effect a junction with the column that, it was expected, would carry the Lahore gate. The rampart itself was inaccessible; but below it ran a lane, which in many places was so narrow that four men could scarcely advance abreast; but, in the midst of a heavy fire, the column dashed on with the utmost intrepidity, clearing the Moree bastion, and inflicting a heavy loss on the enemy, who made a resolute stand at the Caubul gate. Advancing some two hundred yards along the rampart road, formidable obstacles opposed them: a gun, mounted on the rampart itself, and protected by an iron screen, was so depressed as to pour round after round of grape down into the narrow lane, while a gun in advance, protected by a parapet, was likewise fired with deadly effect on the advancing column, while a fusillade of musketry was kept up from the adjoining houses, together with stones and other missiles that were projected upon the devoted heads of the assailants. Again, again, and again did the gallant men advance, and again and again were they mowed down and compelled to desist:—for two hours were repeated attempts made to overcome the defences. Jacob, the gallant commander of the 1st Fusiliers, had already fallen, with many, many others, when the noble Nicolson, who had been with another portion of the column, now joined, and a renewal of the conflict, under his inspiring example, was begun; but a fatal ball laid low that gallant hero; and beside him fell, dangerously wounded, the gallant Greville, of the Fusiliers, and many more. The position of the enemy was too strong, their advantage too great; and as further attempts involved only the sacrifice of gallant men, the column, as well deserving of imperishable glory as if the attacks had been successful, was withdrawn to the Caubul gate. For ten long hours—for it was now two in the afternoon—had these men been under arms, during the greater portion of which they had been exposed to a murderous fire. Such were the men who fought for the honour of Old England within the streets of Delhi; and who, day after day for the ensuing week, fought on until the whole city was in their possession; but for whom it has not been thought worthy to accord a special medal to commemorate this glorious achievement, so truly arduous in its accomplishment, and so beneficial in its results.

K

22.—MUTINOUS SEPOYS.

THIS Sketch represents an interior of one of the batteries, in which are a party of rebel troops. The costume in which these mutineers fought was their usual native dress, upon which were buckled the British accoutrements. This dress consists of a closely-fitting linen jacket, open at the side of the breast, the Mussulman having the opening on the left, the Hindoo on the right. Round their loins a long strip of unbleached cloth, which is wound tightly round and the ends simply tucked in,—this *dhotey* was always worn by the Sepoy beneath his pantaloons, as was the white jacket beneath his regimental coat ; on his head he wore a common white linen skull-cap, and occasionally a turban twisted loosely round his temples, with one end hanging down his back. Frequently, however, the regiments before Delhi turned out in their red coats, with the colours flying and the bands playing ; on one occasion a regiment from the Bareilly brigade marched out, and the well-known music of " Cheer boys, cheer," was wafted by the breeze to the British camp. The Sepoys wear a necklace of white beads, which on the native officers are of gold. In the Sketch, the stout mutineer reposing on his cot is a subadar, or native sergeant-major, as is also the one on the horse, which is caparisoned after the native fashion, and has its mane and legs stained a bright orange-colour.

The Sepoys that composed the Bengal army were a fine body of men ; and it was with a view to secure the tallest and the finest-looking men, that one class—viz., those who came from Oude—were principally selected,—men of high caste, and exceedingly bigoted in their religious views, and which is assigned by many as the main cause of the mutiny having extended so rapidly, as the majority of the army was of one caste, and, it may be said, of one family. The men are tall, the average height being 5 feet 9 inches ; and it was not unfrequent to see grenadier companies with not a man under 6 feet 1 inch. But though tall, and in many cases powerful, muscular men, yet in weight they are not to be compared with the European ; and this may be specially noticed in the tread of a native and of a British regiment. The former pass by with a sort of shuffling pace, while the latter come by with a heavy solid tramp, that seems to shake the earth.

23.—PRIZE AGENTS EXTRACTING TREASURE.

THE grand assault having terminated successfully, and the entire city of Delhi, after a week's hard street-fighting, being in the hands of the British, the more pleasing task of collecting the spoils was now commenced upon ; and no easy work was it for the Prize Agents to secure for the army the spoils they so richly deserved ; for never was more artfully brought into play the cunning and the skill with which the wealthy men had concealed their treasure. Shawls and such-like spoils were more readily obtained, but coin and jewellery, being more easy to hide, the brain had far more effect in discovering the mines of wealth than had the spade ; for it was by judgement—that instigated the piercing into the most improbable places—that at last some key could be obtained to unravelling the mysteries of Oriental concealment. Added to this, the well-known Eastern accomplishment of lying was practised to an unlimited extent ; but the revolver was soon found to be a means of eliciting truth and bags of rupees simultaneously. Treasure was often found in walls duly plastered over, in staircases, between the roof and the beams, and not unfrequently sunk some twenty feet down into the ground, in spots where it was the least expected.

The Sketch represents a scene that occurred. A report had reached the ear of one of the Prize Agents, who of course had offered a large per-centage to those who gave accurate information, that a certain wealthy man had concealed several lakhs of rupees in a certain house. Search was made, but unsuccessfully, the man swearing by everything in creation that he had not a fraction of a rupee concealed. Threats of the rope at last brought out the intelligence that he had some 50,000 rupees in a certain place, but that that was all his wealth. This was speedily extracted, and he was released, when tidings came again that he had not disgorged one quarter of his treasure ; so again was he seized, and, with a revolver at his head, he accounted on the spot for another 50,000, which was as speedily extracted as the former ; but the Prize Agent, convinced that he was still lying, and finding threats unavailing, resolved to establish a little more alarm, placed him as a target, and vowed he would let fly if the fellow did not at once acknowledge where he had concealed the remainder. Still trusting to lies, and little imagining the Prize Agent would keep his word, he again swore most resolutely that he had been disgorged of every pice, and that he really and positively had no more ; upon which the Prize Agent, levelling his revolver, let fly, but purposely avoided hitting him, allowing the bullet to sing within a few inches of his ear. Seeing that the Agent was in earnest, down went the terrified native on his knees, and declared that he would point out where 100,000 rupees were, if his life only was spared. By such devices large sums were discovered ; but probably one-twentieth of the actual wealth of Delhi was never obtained to reward the captors for the many weeks of privation, danger, and death that they were exposed to ere the city fell into their possession.

24.—CAPTURE AND DEATH OF THE SHAHZADAHS.

ONE of the many acts that distinguished the career of the gallant Hodson has already been illustrated in these pages; the next most important feat which made his name so prominently conspicuous, was his capture of the King of Delhi. From information obtained through spies, it was ascertained that the King had taken refuge at Humayon's tomb, about seven miles from Delhi, with a large armed force: Hodson, with fifty troopers of his regiment, sallied forth, resolved, at all hazards, to endeavour to secure him; armed, however, with instructions that he was to promise the King life and freedom from personal indignity. With his small escort he rode up to the neighbourhood of the tomb, and concealing himself and his men in some old building, sent in his emissaries to Zeenat Mahal, the King's favourite wife, with the ultimatum. After two hours of suspense, the emissaries came forth to say the King would deliver himself to Captain Hodson only. Right into the thick of the King's force then rode Hodson boldly, with his small escort, when the King came out of the gateway in his palankeen, and asked if it was "Hodson Bahadoor," and if his life would be spared; upon which Hodson renewed the promises already made, but threatened to shoot the King on the spot if an attempt at a rescue were made. The King then gave up his arms, which Hodson handed to his orderly, still keeping his own sword drawn; and so brought the venerable puppet a prisoner into the city.

This was not sufficient to satisfy Hodson, who was bent upon capturing the two sons and the grandson of the King, viz. Mirza Moghul, Mirza Kheyr Sultan, and Mirza Aboo Bukker, who had taken such a prominent part in the atrocities of the 11th of May. This was an act that required no ordinary amount of daring; for although the King himself had authority sufficient to check the turbulence of the fanatics who surrounded him, it was a different thing in the case of the sons, who, it was supposed, would offer resistance. But Hodson had the courage to face it, and with 100 picked men of his regiment, and accompanied by his second in command, M'Dowell, of the 2nd Fusiliers, he rode again, on the following morning, to within a short distance of the tomb, and sent in emissaries to say the sons must surrender, and surrender unconditionally, which, after a very considerable delay, they accordingly did, feeling confident that, sooner or later, they must be taken, and imagining that, like the King, their lives would be spared. But this was the moment that called for coolness and judgement on the part of Hodson, as, though the sons delivered themselves up, the crowd of fanatics, numbering some 6,000, seemed disposed to prevent it, and a collision was impending, when, by a dexterous movement of his troop, the cart, drawn by bullocks, upon which the sons were seated, was separated from the crowd, which gradually and sullenly fell back towards Humayon's tomb.

Ten troopers were sent on with the cart, and, with the rest of his men, Hodson rode after the mob, and, leaving his party at the gateway, with M'Dowell and four men, rode right up the steps into the archway where the rebels had assembled, and ordered them to lay down their arms. "There was a murmur,—he reiterated his command, and (God knows why), I never can understand it," wrote the gallant but unfortunate M'Dowell, "they commenced doing so." There the party remained for two hours collecting the arms, and in full belief that they would be rushed upon; but a cool, bold front deterred the rebels from the attempt. Carts were then procured, and loaded with the weapons; when Hodson and his troop quietly withdrew, the crowd following them closely. Then, galloping after the King's sons, Hodson caught them up just in time; for the crowd, which had followed them, had increased in numbers, and their gestures and movements indicated an attempt at rescue. Not a moment was to be lost,—Hodson and his small party were but as a log in the ocean; so, addressing rapidly a few words to his men, he himself removed all the object of a rescue, by at once shooting the three blood-thirsty scoundrels, whose bodies, flung on to the cart, were then conveyed into the city, and exposed in the most public place, on the very spot where they had themselves, three months previously, directed and witnessed the butchery of unoffending women and children.

25.—WOUNDED OFFICERS AT SIMLA.

SIMLA is a sanatarium in the Himalayahs, and is situated on a range of mountains about 7,500 feet above the level of the sea; but there are many houses perched upon a loftier range, at a level of 8,000 feet. It is at a distance of forty miles from the plains, the old road from which first ascends to Kussowlie, and attains the 7,500 feet in a length of nine miles: it then descends again to Subathoo, and by continual ascents and descents at last reaches Simla, which has become the most fashionable of all the summer residences in the Himalayahs. The houses are principally built in the neighbourhood of the bazar, contiguous to which are the church, reading-rooms, assembly-rooms, theatre, &c.; but for two miles in either direction, on every accessible spot where a structure could be built, have small rustic dwellings been perched.

The roads are all railed in; and throughout the length of Simla, which extends over four miles, is tolerably level, and upon which, as the pedestrian has good reason to confess, ladies can gallop their horses at full speed. Here the Governor-General resided for several hot seasons, as did also the Commander-in-Chief; and here flock hundreds of officers, with their families, who can be spared from their regiments during those months of the year when military exercises are suspended. Here were assembled scores of officers who had been sent to a bracing and invigorating climate to recover from their wounds, or from the sickness which had fallen on them before Delhi.

The common style of conveyance in the hills is a *jampaun*, which is represented in the Drawing; consisting of a sort of sedan-chair, but carried by four men. It is provided with a shifting top, which consists of four upright rods, supporting a painted canvas roof, and having curtains of black blanketing which is impervious to the wet.

The roads being level, and well railed in, any kind of horse can be ridden at this hill station; but ponies are most preferred; of which excellent ones, born and bred in the inner hills, are greatly prized, as being very sure-footed, and accustomed to traversing, securely, steep and broken roads.

The air of Simla was wonderfully efficacious in restoring the wounded to health: men who were brought up almost lifeless, were to be seen visibly improving day by day; and the weak and emaciated rapidly recovered their strength, and were soon, in many cases, so far restored as to justify their returning to Delhi to take part in the final assault.

26.—WOUNDED MEN AT DUGSHAI.

THE position and characteristics of the station of Dugshai have already been detailed. Situated at a very lofty elevation, it was singularly well adapted for the reception of the sick and wounded soldiers, as the barracks, in consequence of the departure of the 1st Fusiliers, who had occupied them, were now available.

Kussowlie was nearer the plains, but the barracks there had been given up for the use of the wives and families of officers, who, for greater security, had been ordered away from Umballa, that they might enjoy the protection of the small European force, chiefly convalescents, who remained there. Some slight defences had been erected, and the verandahs of the barracks were barricaded, and supplies laid in: so was it at Dugshai. A panic had fallen upon the residents at Simla, in consequence of some misapprehensions, arising from certain unfavourable acts of the Goorkah battalion quartered in the vicinity; upon which a flight was made direct for Dugshai, that safety might be secured behind English bayonets. Ladies, to whom the thought of walking even one mile would have been appalling, now, inspired by fear, actually walked (and in some instances carrying children) the whole distance of nearly forty miles; for the flight was precipitate, and neither conveyances nor horses could be procured. In the Dugshai barracks they sought refuge, and, in full anticipation of the place being assaulted, barricades were erected, and other defences instituted; but the alarm passed away, and the cholera broke out, and the refugees fled back more precipitately than they came. Here men of the Fusiliers, Artillery, Lancers, and other regiments, were to be seen enjoying the truly exhilarating air, after the terrific heat and exposure to which they had been subjected. Wounded men—some desperately, others dangerously, but still able to crawl out—were to be seen sitting together on benches, or lolling on the greensward, fighting again their battles, and now laughing merrily over scenes which were anything but amusing at the time of their occurrence.

The barracks at Dugshai are covered with shingle,—that is, with strips of wood, laid on slate fashion, which, according to the back-wood American system, is the prevailing kind of roofing in the Hills, where timber is plentiful: the walls are of rubble masonry.

Nº 25. WOUNDED OFFICERS AT SIMLA

Capt.ᵗ G. F. Atkinson, del.ᵗ   London Day & Son, Lithographers to the Queen, Gate Street, Lincoln's Inn Fields.   T. Picken, lith.

Nº 26. WOUNDED MEN AT DUGSHAI.